Understanding and Overcoming Cognitive Biases For Lawyers And Law Students

Becoming a Better Lawyer Through Cognitive Science

By E. Scott Fruehwald

This book is intended for educational and informational purposes only.

Copyright 2018

All Rights Reserved

ISBN: 978-1985130135
ISBN: 1985130130

Table of Contents

Preface	v
1. An Introduction to Cognitive Biases	1
2. Optimism Biases	17
3. Negativity Biases	37
4. Biases Concerning Others	49
5. Behavioral Economic Biases	67
6. Cognitive Biases and Practical Reasoning	105
7. Behavioral Legal Ethics	115
8. Special Topics	127
9. Review Exercises on Cognitive Biases	151
10. Review Exercises on Cognitive Biases and Your Professional Life	161

"That is my principal objection to life, I think: It's too easy, when alive, to make perfectly horrible mistakes."

Kurt Vonnegut

If we want to avoid more wars, genocides, and other inhumanities, "it is to the psychology that we should now turn."

Jonathan Glover

[P]rofessional responsibility professors who ignore the psychological underpinnings of moral reasoning are plainly guilty of educational malpractice.

Mary C. Daly

Preface

Did you know that an attorney who represented the New York Times was at the same time helping Harvey Weinstein cover up his sexual misconduct? "One of the nation's most respected lawyers, David Boies, is among those whose work helped Mr. Weinstein try to conceal his abusive behavior."[1] "Mr. Boies's representation posed a conflict of interest, because his firm, Boies Schiller Flexner, was representing The New York Times, the 'leading NY Newspaper,' in libel litigation at the same time."

"Mr. Boies denied that efforts to discredit the Times story reflected such a conflict. In his view, it was 'entirely appropriate to investigate precisely what he'— Mr. Weinstein — 'was accused of doing and to investigate whether there were facts that would rebut those accusations.' And he added, If evidence could be uncovered to convince The Times the charges should not be published, I did not believe, and do not believe, that that would be adverse to The Times's interests.'"

The Times noted that this was a serious ethical conflict: "A lawyer who represents them is prohibited from accepting other matters that would reasonably be considered adverse to their interests without their informed written consent." Mr. Boies defended himself: "Mr. Boies responded in a public statement that his firm had a clause in its retainer agreement with The Times that purported to waive all conflicts of interest on matters unrelated to cases in which the newspaper had retained the firm. But as The Times's leadership pointed out in its own statement, it never contemplated that the firm would contract with investigators to do opposition research on its own reporters."

Why did Mr. Boies engage in conduct that clearly violated written ethical rules? The answer: Cognitive biases (thinking or brain biases)–"a systematic error in thinking that affects the decisions and judgments that people make."[2] Mr. Boies rationalized his actions were not a conflict of interest adverse to the NY Times's interests because of defects in the human thought processes. "While most of us desire to act ethically, 'psychological processes . . . [can] lead people to engage in ethically questionable behaviors that are inconsistent with their own preferred ethics.'"[3] Stated differently, "[W]hen people are thinking about honesty versus dishonesty, it's all about being able, at the moment, to rationalize something and make yourself think that this is actually okay."[4]

Over the past 30 years, cognitive scientists have made enormous advances in understanding how the brain works. In particular, Daniel Kahneman, wrote a book that summarized the decades of work he and his research partner, Amos Tversky, had done on behavioral economics and cognitive biases.[5] Kahmeman's goal in writing the book "was to improve the ability to identify and understand errors of judgment in others and eventually in ourselves, by providing a richer and more precise language to discuss them."[6]

I have written this book to show how cognitive biases and other psychological process affect lawyers. I will discuss how lawyers can use their understanding of cognitive biases to become better and more ethical lawyers. I will then show how lawyers can avoid being manipulated by others through their cognitive biases. I will also explain how lawyers can use cognitive biases in persuasion. Most importantly, I will demonstrate how attorneys can avoid unconscious ethical lapses.

Cognitive biases can affect lawyers in many ways. Cognitive biases can hurt an attorney and her clients. For example, a lawyer may overestimate the chances of winning a case because of a cognitive bias. Similarly, an attorney may attack an opponent on irrelevant grounds because she dislikes the other attorney because of a cognitive bias. Likewise, an attorney might misunderstand what a client is trying to say because of a bias. Moreover, a lawyer may make an ethical slip because she does not realize that an ethical question is involved.

Cognitive biases can also help an attorney. For example, an attorney can use cognitive biases in persuasive writing and oral argument. Similarly, a lawyer can use her knowledge of cognitive biases to better understand her clients, her opponents, judges, and juries.

Many scholars agree that humans can overcome their cognitive biases and improve their thinking and behavior. For example, Greg Lukianoff and Jonathan Haidt are confident that individuals can overcome their brain biases.[7] They write, "For millennia, philosophers have understood that we don't see life as it is; we see a version distorted by our hopes, fears, and other attachments. The Buddha said, 'Our life is the creation of our mind.' Marcus Aurelius said, 'Life itself is but what you deem it.' The quest for wisdom in many traditions begins with this insight. Early Buddhists and the Stoics, for example, developed practices for reducing attachments, thinking more clearly, and finding release from the emotional torments of normal mental life."

Similarly, many scientists argue that we can overcome our cognitive biases to a large extent with training.[8] One study showed that irrationality correlates weakly with I.Q. In other words, "A person with a high I.Q. is about as likely to suffer from dysrationalia as a person with a low I.Q."[9] Later studies have confirmed that "There is also now evidence that rationality, unlike intelligence, can be improved through training." The article concludes, "While there is scant evidence that any sort of 'brain training' has any real-world impact on intelligence, it may well be possible to train people to be more rational in their decision making."

Overcoming cognitive biases can produce amazing results. For example, "Atul Gawande, an accomplished medical professional, recounts the results of an initiative at a major U.S. hospital, in which a test run showed that doctors skipped at least one of only 5 steps in 1/3 of certain surgery cases, after which nurses were given the authority and responsibility to catch doctors missing any steps in a simple checklist aimed at reducing central line infections. In the subsequent 15-month period, infection rates went from 11% to 0%, 8 deaths were avoided and some $2 million in avoidable costs were saved."[10]

The first part of this book (Chapters 1–5) will introduce you to cognitive biases. It will help you understand these biases, show how these biases work in the law and legal profession, and give exercises to help you overcome your cognitive biases. Chapter 6 will go into more depth by showing how the cognitive biases fit into a model of practical reasoning. Chapter 7 will demonstrate how cognitive biases affect legal ethics (behavioral legal ethics). Chapter 8 will present special problems concerning cognitive biases and the legal profession. Chapter 9 will contain additional exercises on cognitive biases in general, and Chapter 10 contains review exercises focused on lawyers and the practice of law.

A key goal of this book is to help you overcome your cognitive biases. The first step in this process is to make you aware of the many cognitive biases that affect all human thinking. An individual cannot overcome a problem unless he or she is aware of it. I go into detail with each major bias so you can understand them better. I have also written exercises

Preface

that require you to recognize the various cognitive biases.

Carefully doing the exercises is essential to recognizing and overcoming your cognitive biases. Studies have shown that people retain much more information and are able to manipulate that information better with active learning, rather than passive learning, such as just reading.

My main way of helping you to overcome your cognitive biases is to change your metacognitive thinking about each bias. (You don't have to be an expert on metacognition to use this book; you just need to be open to new ways of thinking.) Metacognition is thinking about thinking–controlling one's cognitive processes (the actual thinking).[11] More specifically, "[w]e now understand the brain as a network of regions working in concert, and thus, it is perhaps unsurprising that one set of regions (such as the prefrontal cortex: PFC) might process, hierarchically, information arising from lower levels (such as primary sensory regions)."[12] Furthermore, "cognition primarily focuses on the skills needed to perform a task, while metacognition involves the understanding of how a task is performed."[13] Stated more simply, metacognition is like a supercomputer that controls the many functions of a self-driving car, functions which are controlled by smaller computers of their own.

My main method of changing your metaconitive thinking about cognitive biases is to ask you metacognitive questions, which you can use to reflect on your thinking processes. Examples of metacognitive questions include:

1. What skills are most important for a lawyer?
2. What are the strengths and weaknesses of my study techniques? Do I use a variety of study techniques?
3. Do I always have clear goals when I tackle a problem?
4. Do I ask myself whether I have accomplished my goals when I finish studying or finish a task?
5. Do I carefully consider all alternatives, or do I jump to conclusions based on limited evidence? (This last one is very important for overcoming cognitive biases.)

Because this is a practical study, I had originally intended to keep notes to a minimum. However, for obvious reasons, I had to cite to numerous sources. Consequently, I put the notes at the end of the chapters and simplified the citations. You do not have to consult the notes to understand the text. Use the notes if you want to know where to look for more information. I have included links whenever possible.

This book does not take a legal political position on any issue.[14] Rather, its point is to help you overcome your biases and try to view the world from an objective viewpoint. This does not mean that the book has failed if you still have strong legal or political viewpoints when you finish working with it. I do hope, though, that, when you are done with my book, your legal and political viewpoints will be based on rational thinking, rather than cognitive biases.

There is some overlap between this book and my previous book, Overcoming Cognitive Biases: Thinking More Clearly and Avoiding Manipulation by Others. I suggest you read this book if you want to understand cognitive biases and the legal profession. I suggest you read my earlier book if you want to understand cognitive biases in general.

Understanding and Overcoming Cognitive Biases for Lawyers and Law Students

Notes

1. Deboral L. Rhode, *David Boies's Egregious Involvement With Harvey Weinstein* (Nov. 9, 2017). [https://www.nytimes.com/2017/11/09/opinion/david-boies-harvey-weinstein.html]

2. Kendra Cherry, *What is a Cognitive Bias? Defintions and Examples*, VeryWell (May 26, 2016). [https://www.verywell.com/what-is-a-cognitive-bias-2794963]

3. Jennifer K. Robbennolt & Jean R. Sternlight, *Behavioral Legal Ethics*, https://papers.ssrn.com/sol3/papers.cfm?abstract_id=2248137 at 8 (2013).

4. *Behavioral Ethics*, https://www.pbs.org/wnet/religionandethics/2014/06/27/june-27-2014-behavioral-ethics/23445/ (June 27, 2014), *quoting*, Dan Ariely.

5. Daniel Kahneman, Thinking, Fast and Slow (2011).

6. *Id.* at 4.

7. Greg Lukianoff and Jonathan Haidt, The Coddling of the American Mind, The Atlantic (Sept 15 2015). [http://www.theatlantic.com/magazine/archive/2015/09/] I will deal with their ideas in greater depth in Chapter Three.

8. David Z. Hambrick & Alexander P. Burgoyne, *The Difference Between Rationality and Intelligence*, N.Y. Times (Sept. 16, 2016) [http://www.nytimes.com/2016/09/18/opinion/sunday/the-difference-between-rationality-and-intelligence.html?rref=collection%2Fcolumn%2FGray%20Matter&action=click&contentCollection=Opinion&module=Collection&region=Marginalia&src=me&version=column&pgtype=article&_r=1]; *see also* Carey K. Morewedge et.al., *Debiasing Decisions: Improved Decision Making With a Single Training Intervention*, 2 Policy Insights from the Behavioral and Brain Sciences 129–140 (2015).

9. Hambrick & Burgoyne, *supra*.

10. Wikipedia: Cognitive Bias Mitigation, https://en.wikipedia.org/wiki/Cognitive_bias_mitigation.

11. Marcel V.J. Veenman et.al, *Metacognition and Learning: Conceptual and Methodological Considerations*, 1 METACOGNITION LEARNING 3, 6 (2006) [http://www.csuchico.edu/~nschwartz/Veenman%20Metacognition.pdf]; Michael Hunter Schwartz, *Teaching Law by Design: How Learning Theory and Instructional Design Can Inform and Reform Law Teaching*, 38 SAN DIEGO L. REV. 347, 376 (2001). More specifically, metacognition regulates learning through a cognitive regulatory loop. First, metacognition monitors the learning process. Then, based on that monitoring, metacognition controls the learning process. Thus, metacognition consists of two main subdivisions: knowledge of cognition and regulation of cognition (control).

12. Stephan M. Fleming & Raymond J. Dolan, *The Neural Basis of Metacognitive Ability*, 367 PHIL. TRANS. R. SOC. B 1338, 1338 (2012). [http://ukpmc.ac.uk/articles/PMC3318765]

13. Anthony S. Niedwiecki, *Lawyers and Learning: A Metacognitive Approach to Legal Education*, 13 WIDENER L. REV. 33, 42-43 (2006).

14. At times, my problems do have to take a political view so that you can see the fault in political reasoning based on cognitive biases. However, by doing so, I don't mean to advocate any political or ideological position. They are just examples and exercises.

Chapter One
An Introduction to Cognitive Biases

<u>Chapter Goals</u>.
1. To introduce the cognitive biases.
2. To introduce brainstorming.
3. To introduce the two main types of thinking: intuition and reasoning.
4. To introduce heuristics.
5. To explain the effect of emotions on reasoning.
6. To give you tools for overcoming cognitive biases: reflection, evaluation, self-monitoring, and problem-solving.

I. An Introduction to Cognitive Biases

Cognitive biases (thinking or brain biases) are "systematic error[s] in thinking that affect[] the decisions and judgments that people make."[1] The human thinking process is imperfect. Like the other parts of the human body, the brain evolved. Parts of our brains today are remnants of the brains our early ancestors had, brains which had developed to survive under very different conditions from today. Evolution is not history; it is what humans are today. These remnants produce cognitive biases–ways of thinking that are different from reality.

Here is a list of common mental biases:[2]

1. Anchoring: "The tendency to rely too heavily, or 'anchor', on one trait or piece of information when making decisions (usually the first piece of information that we acquire on that subject)."
2. Availability heuristic: "The tendency to overestimate the likelihood of events with greater 'availability' in memory, which can be influenced by how recent the memories are or how unusual or emotionally charged they may be."
3. Bandwagon effect: "The tendency to do (or believe) things because many other people do (or believe) the same."
4. Base-rate effect: "The tendency to ignore base rate information (generic, general information) and focus on specific information (information only pertaining to a certain case)."
5. Bias blind spot: "The tendency to see oneself as less biased than other people, or to be able to identify more cognitive biases in others than in oneself."
6. Blaming: Focusing on the other person as the source of negative feelings, and refusing to take responsibility for changing yourself.
7. Catastrophizing: Believing that what has happened or will happen will be so awful and unbearable that you won't be able to stand it.
8. Confirmation bias: "The tendency to search for, interpret, focus on and remember infor-

mation in a way that confirms one's preconceptions."
9. Curse of knowledge: "When better-informed people find it extremely difficult to think about problems from the perspective of lesser-informed people."
10. Dichotomous thinking: Viewing events or people in all-or-nothing terms.
11. Discounting positives: Claiming that the positive things you or others do are trivial.
12. Empathy gap: "The tendency to underestimate the influence or strength of feelings, in either oneself or others."
13. Emotional reasoning: Letting your feelings guide your interpretation of reality.
14. Endowment effect: "The fact that people often demand much more to give up an object than they would be willing to pay to acquire it."
15. Essentialism: "Categorizing people and things according to their essential nature, in spite of variations."
16. Expectation bias: "The tendency for experimenters to believe, certify, and publish data that agree with their expectations for the outcome of an experiment, and to disbelieve, discard, or downgrade the corresponding weightings for data that appear to conflict with those expectations."
17. Fortune-telling: Predicting the future negatively: things will get worse, or there is danger ahead.
18. Framing effect: "Drawing different conclusions from the same information, depending on how that information is presented."
19. Functional fixedness: "Limits a person to using an object only in the way it is traditionally used."
20. Gambler's fallacy: "The tendency to think that future probabilities are altered by past events, when in reality they are unchanged."
21. Halo effect: "The tendency for a person's positive or negative traits to 'spill over' from one personality area to another in others' perceptions of them."
22. Hindsight bias: "Sometimes called the 'I-knew-it-all-along' effect, the tendency to see past events as being predictable at the time those events happened."
23. Hyperbolic discounting: "The tendency for people to have a stronger preference for more immediate payoffs relative to later payoffs."
24. Identifiable victim effect: "The tendency to respond more strongly to a single identified person at risk than to a large group of people at risk."
25. Illusion of control: "The tendency to overestimate one's degree of influence over other external events."
26. Illusory correlation: "Inaccurately perceiving a relationship between two unrelated events."
27. Inability to disconfirm: Rejecting any evidence or arguments that might contradict your negative thoughts.
28. In-group bias: "The tendency for people to give preferential treatment to others they perceive to be members of their own groups."
29. Labeling. Assigning global negative traits to yourself and others.
30. Loss aversion: "The disutility of giving up an object is greater than the utility associated with acquiring it."
31. Mere exposure effect: "The tendency to express undue liking for things merely because of familiarity with them."

An Introduction to Cognitive Biases

32. Mind reading: Assuming that you know what people think without having sufficient evidence of their thoughts.
33. Negative filtering: Focusing almost exclusively on the negatives and seldom noticing the positives.
34. Normalcy bias: "The refusal to plan for, or react to, a disaster which has never happened before."
35. Optimism bias: "The tendency to be over-optimistic, overestimating favorable and pleasing outcomes."
36. Ostrich effect: "Ignoring an obvious (negative) situation."
37. Overconfidence effect: "Excessive confidence in one's own answers to questions."
38. Overgeneralizing: Perceiving a global pattern of negatives on the basis of a single incident.
39. Planning fallacy: "The tendency to underestimate task-completion times."
40. Projection bias: "The tendency to unconsciously assume that others (or one's future selves) share one's current emotional states, thoughts and values."
41. Reactive devaluation: "Devaluing proposals only because they purportedly originated with an adversary."
42. Self-serving bias: "The tendency to claim more responsibility for successes than failures."
43. Semmelweis reflex: "The tendency to reject new evidence that contradicts a paradigm."
44. Sunken cost fallacy: "A cost that has already been incurred and cannot be recovered."
45. Status quo bias: "The tendency to like things to stay relatively the same."
46. Subjective validation: "Perception that something is true if a subject's belief demands it to be true. Also assigns perceived connections between coincidences."
47. What if?: You keep asking a series of questions about "what if" something happens, and you fail to be satisfied with any of the answers.

I realize that you are just at the beginning of your understanding of cognitive biases, but try to answer the following questions.

Exercise I-1

1. Do you recognize any of these biases in your everyday thinking? Can you see how they might have affected your thinking? Would you have done anything differently if you had been aware of the bias?
2. Have any of these biases affected your performance as a lawyer? How?
2. Have you seen any of these biases in others recently? How did they affect the person's thinking? (include journalists and commentators you have seen on tv and articles you have read.)
3. Which of these biases do you think are most important for you to avoid? In general? Based on your individual self? For lawyers?

If you struggled with these, don't be frustrated. I will deal with each of these biases in detail in later chapters.

Of these biases, the most dangerous ones for lawyers are probably the overconfidence effect, the bias blind spot, blaming, the curse of knowledge, the expectation bias, the illusion of control, mind reading, the projection bias, and the self-serving bias because these biases involve "our excessive confidence in what we believe we know, and our apparent inability to acknowledge the full extent of our ignorance and the uncertainty of the world we live in."[3]

As you can see from the above exercises, humans frequently suffer from cognitive biases in their everyday lives. This is nothing to be ashamed of. People on all sides of political and ideological arguments suffer from these biases–both conservatives and liberals, republicans, democrats, and independents. My point is that you will become a better thinker if you can recognize these biases in yourself.

So, let's begin by acknowledging that we have limitations.[4] As Kahneman has stated, "you must accept that they are true about you."[5] In this way, ironically, we will become better decision-makers.

Of course, the above are possible biases. After you identify a possible cognitive bias, you need to evaluate whether it is actually affecting your thinking. The way to do this is to identify the possible cognitive bias, then objectively and critically evaluate if and how it is affecting your thinking.

This is much like brainstorming–a creativity exercise. The first step of brainstorming is to write down all the possible solutions to a problem without being critical. In the second step, you should be critical of any solutions that are wrong, won't work, or are impractical. The classical example of brainstorming is to think up all the uses for a brick.

Let's start with a simple cognitive bias–the functional fitness bias–to help you understand how biases work. The functional fitness bias–"Limits a person to using an object only in the way it is traditionally used."

In the exercises below, first write down all the possible uses of the object, then critically assess whether those uses are practical.

1. A brick.
2. A pencil
3. A baseball.
4. A toothbrush.
5. A shower cap.
6. Look around the room and identify other objects you can use for this exercise.
7. Imagine you are lost in the woods. Picture the objects you can use to survive.

The television show "MacGyver" is an excellent example of overcoming this bias.

Note: Cognitive biases are different than logical fallacies: "A logical fallacy is an error in logical argumentation (e.g. ad hominem attacks, slippery slopes, circular arguments, appeal to force, etc.). A cognitive bias, on the other hand, is a genuine deficiency or limitation in our thinking—a flaw in judgment that arises from errors of memory, social attribution, and miscalculations (such as statistical errors or a false sense of probability)."[6]

II. Intuition Versus Reasoning

To more fully understand cognitive biases, you must understand the two types of human thinking: intuition and reasoning. Professor Kahneman calls these System 1 and System 2.

> System 1 operates automatically and quickly, with little or no effort and no sense of voluntary control. System 2 allocates attention to the effortful mental activities that demand it, including complex computations. The operations of System 2 are often associated with the subjective experience of agency, choice, and concentration.[7]

In other words, System 1 is unconscious, intuitive thought (automatic pilot), while slower System 2 is conscious, rational thinking (effortful system). "System 1 is designed to jump to conclusions from little evidence–and it is not designed to know the size of its jumps."[8] System 2 is the executive, and it can undertake critical thinking.

An example of System 1 thinking is driving. Are you conscious of everything you do when you drive? Of course not. You watch for cars, stop for red lights, even change lanes without thinking about it. It is almost like you have a self-driving car, but the computer guiding the car is in your head. However, this changes when you are trying to find a new address using a map. This task is effortful because it requires complex computations. You must think how to get to the address using a map–a symbolic representation. You must then translate the map into what you are seeing when you are driving. You then follow landmarks and street signs, which correspond to what is on the map.

When we are awake, most of our actions are controlled automatically by System 1. The mind cannot consciously perform the thousands of complex tasks per day that human functioning requires. System 2 is normally in a low-effort mode. "Most impressions and thoughts arise in your conscious experience without you knowing how they got there."[9] System 2 activates when System 1 cannot deal with a task–when more detailed processing is needed; only System 2 can construct thoughts in a step-by-step fashion. In addition, it continuously monitors human behavior. Also, "System 1 continuously generates suggestions for System 2; impressions, intuitions, intentions, and feelings. . . When all goes smoothly, , which is most of the time, System 2 adopts the suggestions of System 1 with little or no modification."[10]

The interactions of Systems 1 and 2 are usually highly efficient. However, System 1 is prone to biases ("biases of intuition)" and errors, and System 2 is often lazy. A central purpose of System 2 is to "overcome the impulses of System 1"–self-control.[11] The brain employs "executive control" to override the habitual responses of System 1.[12]

System 2 has limited capacity.[13] Thus, humans must focus their attention to the task at hand in order to think effectively. This requires effort. "Effort is required to maintain simultaneously in memory several ideas that require separate actions, or that need to be combined according to a rule."[14] Also, switching from one task to another or working under time pressure requires effort.[15]

Thus, "effortful thinking also requires self-control" (discipline).[16] Some people can assert self-control for long periods, which is called flow–"a state of concentration so deep that they lose their sense of time, of themselves, of their problems."[17] With flow, one does not have to exert self-control to maintain attention because the activities are absorbing.[18] In other words, you should choose mental actives that are interesting to you.

However, effort is required for much System 2 thinking. Those who do not assert effort will come up with superficial answers, while those who do will produce correct and complex answers. As Profesor Kahneman has declared,

> "Lazy" is a harsh judgment about the self-monitoring of these young people and their System 2, but it does not seem to be unfair. Those who avoid the sin of intellectual sloth could be called "engaged." They are more alert, more intellectually active, less willing to be satisfied with superficially attractive answers, more skeptical about their intuitions. . . . [They are] more rational![19]

In sum, "self-control requires attention and effort."[20] Hint: effort is physical in that it requires energy–glucose. Therefore, when you have trouble concentrating, eat something with glucose![21] Similarly, avoid making tough decisions when you are angry, sad, or tired.

Dealing with intuitions. Here is some general advise on dealing with intuitions: Be critical of your intuitions. First, try to recognize when you have made a decision based on an intuition. If you find yourself rationalizing, it is a sign that you have made the decision using intuition based on cognitive biases and you are now trying to rationalize that intuition. Then, test the intuition through deliberative reasoning and reflection. Ask why you came up with that intuition. Check to see whether your intuition can be backed up by your System 2. Get all the facts, and consider all alternatives. Ask what others would say about your intuition. (Your boss at work. A teacher concerning an assignment. A spouse concerning a purchase.) Consult with others about your intuitions, especially when it is an important decision. Reward yourself when you slow down your thinking.

Exercise I-2A

1. Do Kahneman's System 1 and System 2 reflect how you think? Do you ever think about your thinking process? Do you feel that your thinking would improve if you did?
2. How do Systems 1 and 2 reflect on how you think as a lawyer? How much does intuition affect your legal reasoning?
3. Write down situations in your life where System 1 kicks in. How aware are you of what you are doing? One time, I sat down to tie my shoes. For a few seconds I couldn't think about how I tied my shoes. The process was so automatic to me that I would have to think through it before I explained shoe tying to anyone else. This realization gave me a very strange feeling. Do you think about how you tie your shoes? Do you think about how you eat? Do you think about how you get out of bed? Brush your teeth? Have you ever found yourself driving to work when you were actually going some place else because driving to work was automatic?
4. Think about everything you do in your everyday life that involves System 2. How much effort do you expend on these tasks?
5. Do you jump to conclusions too often? Does overusing System 1 cause you problems? Don't be a "cognitive miser."[22]
6. Habits are System 1 thinking. Do you have any bad habits? How did you change a bad

An Introduction to Cognitive Biases

habit?

Exercise I-2B

Are the following examples of System 1 or System 2 thinking?

1. A manager chooses a pinch hitter based on statistics.
2. Martha thinks she has chosen a reliable car because it has a beautiful exterior.
3. A coach put in a basketball player because she thought it was time for her to get "hot."
4. Juan choose Eastern Parkway, rather than his usual rout (the expressway), because he has observed that the expressway usually backs up when it is raining.
5. Flo wanted to go to the best college in the state. She choose to go to Eastern State because it had a pretty campus.
6. Leroy wanted to buy a reliable car. He spent hours studying *Consumer Reports*.
7. Despite the fact that the maps showed that the east face of the mountain was easier to climb, the team leader choose the north face based on a gut feeling. Two climbers were injured on the north face.
8. Wanda voted not guilty because she thought that such a handsome man could not have killed his wife.
9. On the way to work, Martha turned onto Walnut Street. This was her usual route.
10. The witness thought that the gun shot came from in front of him, but he was wrong because it had echoed off a building.
11. You come up with a strategy for a case after reading the file several times and reflecting for several days.
12. You decide that your client is not guilty because she is well-educated.
13. You advise your client about a settlement offer because of a gut feeling.
14. You advise your client about a settlement offer after you have put the facts of the case into a formula developed by statisticians.
15. You advise your client that he has a strong chance of winning the case at the end of the initial interview.
16. You initially thought that your client was not guilty. However, later evidence suggests that your client is guilty. However, you still think your client is not guilty.
17. A wealthy client has asked you to help her with estate planning. You have never done estate planning before, but you think you can handle the case.
18. You represent two clients who are creditors in the same bankruptcy. After checking the rules and relevant cases, you believe there is no ethical problem.

Answers

1. System 2. He used his rational judgment based on statistics.
2. System 1. She has based her choice on intuition. A beautiful car says nothing about reliability.
3. System 1. She made a guess based on instinct.
4. Since he based his decision on observation, Juan was using System 2.

5. System 1. A pretty campus does not mean that a college has a good educational program.
6. System 2. He based his decision on evidence.
7. Obviously, System 1.
8. System 1.
9. System 1.
10. System 1.
11. System 2.
12. System 1. Halo effect.
13. System 1.
14. System 2.
15. System 1.
16. System 1. Expectation bias.
17. System 1. Overconfidence effect.
18. System 1. This is a problem that is best dealt with through behavioral legal ethics. (Chapter Seven)

Before ending this part, I want to be clear that System 1 thinking is not always or even usually faulty. If it were, mankind would have become extinct in primitive times. As Kahneman declared, "System 1 is indeed the origin of much that we do wrong, but it is also the origin of most of what we do right–which is most of what we do."[23] What you need to recognize is that System 1 can lead to errors, so you should use System 2 to monitor System 1. Of course, this requires "a considerable investment of effort."[24]

Kahneman also discusses heuristics–"a simple procedure that helps find adequate, though often imperfect, answers to difficult questions."[25] Stated differently, heuristics are rules of thumb that humans use to answer difficult questions, causing "predictable biases (systematic errors) in their predictions."[26] Heuristics, a function of System 1, allow humans to act fast, but they can also lead to wrong conclusions (biases) because they sometimes substitute an easier question for the one asked.[27] A lazy System 2 often adopts the easy heuristic answer of System 1 without close inspection.[28]

A type of heuristic is the halo effect–"the tendency to like (or dislike) everything about a person–including things you have not observed."[29] A simple example is rating a baseball player as good at pitching because he is handsome and athletic.

Another example of a heuristic bias is when judgments are influenced by an uninformative number (an anchor), which results from an associative activation in System 1. People are influenced when they consider a particular value for an unknown number before estimating that number. The estimate for a number then stays close to the anchor. For example, two groups estimated Gandhi's age when he died. The first group were initially asked whether he was more than 114; a second group was asked whether he was 35 or older. The first group estimated a higher number for when he died than the second one.

Kahneman believes that heuristics are not the basis of expertise: accurate intuitions of experts derive from prolonged practice, not heuristics.[30] He quotes Herbert Simon on chess masters: "The situation has provided a cue. This cue has given the expert access to information stored in memory, and the information provides the answer. [Expert] [i]ntuition is nothing more or nothing less than recognition."[31] In other words, "[v]alid intuitions develop when experts have learned to recognize familiar elements in a new situation and to act in a manner that is appropriate to it."[32]

In sum, heuristics cause biases because they give an easy answer to a difficult question.[33]

III. Emotions and Cognitive Biases

Professor Kahnemen believes that emotions play a role in how humans think, affecting intuition and thus cognitive biases.[34] "[W]hen we are uncomfortable and unhappy, we lose touch with our intuition."[35]

Emotions often help humans make better decisions. "Damasio and his colleagues have observed that people who do not display the appropriate emotions before they decide, sometimes because of brain damage, also have an impaired ability to make good decisions."[36]

However, emotions can also have negative effects on decision-making. The "affect heuristic" (gut decision) is "a mental shortcut that allows people to make decisions and solve problems quickly and efficiently, in which current emotion—fear, pleasure, surprise, etc.—influences decisions."[37] It speeds up decision-making.[38] "Researchers have found that if we have pleasant feelings about something, we see the benefits as high and the risks as low, and vice versa."[39] While this time-saving heuristic helped our ancestors survive when they faced a life or death situation, it can interfere with your decision-making.

Examples.
A heart (positive emotion).
A puppy (positive emotion).
Cancer (negative emotion).
Discrimination (negative emotion).

I will talk about the effect of emotions on our thinking processes throughout this book. For now, try to be aware when emotions are affecting your decisions. In this case, slow down and avoid snap judgments. Use a thorough problem-solving process to check if your intuitions are correct, or whether they are causing you to come up with a bad solution.

IV. Some Tools for Overcoming Cognitive Biases:
Reflection, Evaluation, Self-Monitoring
and Problem Solving

Here are some tools that will help you overcome your cognitive biases:

Reflection

Reflection is "an active thought process aimed at understanding and subsequent improvement."[40] Furthermore, "reflection facilitates [thinkers] to draw from their previous practic[al] experience and to apply that which is relevant to new and unfamiliar [] situations."[41]

Understanding and Overcoming Cognitive Biases for Lawyers and Law Students

Being a reflective thinker starts at the metacognitive level. Metacognition involves "knowledge about one's own knowledge and knowledge about one's own performance."[42] It allows "learners to understand and monitor their cognitive processes."[43] "Metacognition involves the understanding of how a task is performed."[44] Stated differently, "'Metacognition refers to awareness of one's own knowledge—what one does and doesn't know—and one's ability to understand, control, and manipulate one's cognitive processes. It includes knowing when and where to use particular strategies for learning and problem solving as well as how and why to use specific strategies. Metacognition is the ability to use prior knowledge to plan a strategy for approaching a learning task, take necessary steps to problem solve, reflect on and evaluate results, and modify one's approach as needed."[45] In sum, metacognition is one's inner voice or inner critic, and a self-regulated thinker develops her inner voice.

Your inner voice asks you questions about what you are learning or doing. It asks you to relate your learning to what you have learned previously. It asks you to criticize what you have learned or done. It asks you about the implications and consequences of what you have read. It also makes you think about the alternatives to what you have read or done. It forces you to be an active, adult thinker, rather than a child thinker who only passively thinks and overrelies on her System 1.

One way to become a reflective learner is to keep a journal and write in it every night.

Evaluation (Learning from Your Mistakes)

Part of overcoming biases is the ability to learn from your mistakes. Do you think about what went wrong when you have made a bad decision? Evaluating a project once it is done will help you recognize your cognitive biases.

With evaluation, you consider how well your learning or problem-solving process worked. Did I come to the correct solution? Did I consider all alternatives? Was my process as efficient as possible? What have I learned to improve my processes in the future?

Self-Monitoring

Self-monitoring is a type of evaluation that occurs while you are reading, learning, or problem solving. It is concentrating on how well you are doing a process while you are doing it. It helps you avoid mistakes and adopt the most efficient process. It also helps you slow down your thinking.

Questions: Reflection, Evaluation, and Self-Monitoring

1. Do you reflect on what you have read?
2. Did you reflect on what you have learned in class in college and law school?
3. Do you think about alternative solutions while problem solving?
4. Do you think of applications for what you have learned?
5. Do you evaluate your problem-solving process?
6. Do you criticize how well you have done an assignment (work or school) when you are finished?

An Introduction to Cognitive Biases

7. Do you self-monitor your reading process?
8. Do you self-monitor your learning process?
9. Do you self-monitor your problem-solving process?
10. Do you self-monitor your work process?
11. What kind of study habits did you use in school? Were these effective ways to learn?

I bet most of your answers to these questions were no because you have not previously been taught to do these things. However, your thinking process and ability to overcome biases will improve dramatically if you add these processes to your metacognitive repertoire.

Problem Solving

Problem solving is a <u>step-by-step</u> process that leads from identifying the problem to a reasonable solution. Problem-solving methods differ based on the problem. Here is a general model for problem solving: 1) Identify the problem, 2) Define the problem, 3) Form a strategy, 4) Organize information, 5) Solve the problem (including monitoring and reflecting on your progress), 6) Evaluate the solution.[46] Here is my approach to legal problem solving: 1) Gather facts, 2) Frame issues, 3) Research, 4) Brief (analyze) cases, 5) Synthesis, 6) Develop problem-solving strategy, 7) Apply law to facts, 8) Form conclusions, 9) Write up, 10) Evaluate. With both these methods, you will have many substeps in each step.

Performing tasks, including problem solving, involves three recursive stages: forethought, performance, and reflection.[47] In other words, think about doing the task, perform the task, reflect on what you have done. Most people only do the performance stage.

Questions: Problem Solving

1. Do you have a problem-solving method(s)? Can you see why having problem-solving methods is important?
2. Do you break tasks into parts and subparts (steps)? Doesn't breaking tasks into parts and subparts make them easier to do? Doesn't breaking tasks into parts and subparts make it more likely you will come up with the best solution?
3. Do you employ the three stages of task performance–forethought, performance, and reflection? Can you see how employing all three stages will help you solve problems better?

V. Wrap-Up Exercises

1. Dilbert cartoons by Scott Adams are a rich source of cognitive biases. (Some of them are available online.) Look through some Dilbert cartoons and identify the cognitive biases.
2. The cable news networks are a rich source of cognitive biases. Look at some cable news shows and try to identify the cognitive biases. Look at both conservative and liberal networks.
3. When you watch ads on television, try to determine which cognitive bias(es) the ad is using to sell its product.
4. Always be on the lookout for cognitive biases in your education, your law practice, and your life.

Understanding and Overcoming Cognitive Biases for Lawyers and Law Students

Preview

In the following chapters I will deal in detail with the most common cognitive biases:

Chapter 2: Optimism Biases
Chapter 3: Negativity Biases
Chapter 4: Biases Concerning Others
Chapter 5: Behavioral Economic Biases

An Introduction to Cognitive Biases

Notes

1. Kendra Cherry, *What is a Cognitive Bias? Defintions and Examples*, VeryWell (May 26, 2016). [https://www.verywell.com/what-is-a-cognitive-bias-2794963]

2. I complied this list from an article in Wikipedia and an article by Greg Lukianoff and Jonathan Haidt. I used the list in Wikipedia because it was a comprehensive list. I double-checked the cites in Wikipedia. The quotes: *Wikipedia: List of Cognitive Biases*. [https://en.wikipedia.org/wiki/List_of_cognitive_biases]; the rest: Greg Lukianoff and Jonathan Haidt, The Coddling of the American Mind, The Atlantic (Sept 15 2015). [http://www.theatlantic.com/magazine/archive/2015/09/]

3. Daniel Kahneman, Thinking, Fast and Slow 14 (2011).

4. Kahneman notes that even highly intelligent people are subject to biases. Rationality and intelligence are separate things. Biases are a failure of rationality, not intelligence. *Id.* at 49.

5. *Id.* at 57.

6. George Dvorsky, *The 12 cognitive biases that prevent you from being rational*, io9 (Jan. 9, 2013). [http://io9.gizmodo.com/5974468/the-most-common-cognitive-biases-that-prevent-you-from-being-rational]

7. Kahneman, *supra* at 20-21.

8. *Id.* at 209.

9. *Id.* at 4.

10. *Id.* at 24.

11. *Id.* at 26.

12. *Id.* at 36-7.

13. *Id.* at 35; Duane F. Shell et.al., The Unified Learning Model: How Motivational, Cognitive, and Neurobiological Sciences Inform Best Teaching Practices 11, 20 (2010).

14. Kahneman, *supra* at 36.

15. *Id.* at 37.

16. *Id.* at 40.

17. *Id.*

18. *Id.* at 41.

19. *Id.* at 46 (emphasis added).

20. *Id.* at 41.

21. *Id.* at 43. You probably have seen the Snicker's commercial with the saying "You get cranky when you're hungry." More accurately, you can't think clearly when you're hungry.

22. Richard F. West et.al., *Cognitive Sophistication Does Not Attenuate the Bias Blind Spot*, 103 Journal of Personality and Social Psychology 506, 507 (2012). [http://keithstanovich.com/Site/Research_on_Reasoning_files/West_Stanovich_JPSP2012.pdf]

23. Kahneman, *supra* at 416.

24. *Id.* at 417.

25. *Id.* at 98

26. *Id.* at 7.

27. *Id.* at 98.

28. *Id.* at 99.

29. *Id.* at 82.

30. *Id.* at 11.

31. *Id.*

32. *Id.* at 12.

33. *Id.*

34. *Id.*

35. *Id.* at 69.

36. *Id.* at 139.

37. *Wikipedia: Affect Heuristic*. [https://en.wikipedia.org/wiki/Affect_heuristic]

38. *Affect Heuristic: How our Emotions Speed Up Decision-Making*, Being Human. [http://www.beinghuman.org/article/affect-heuristic]

39. *Id.*

40. Jennifer York-Barr et.al., Reflective Practice to Improve Schools: An Action Guide for Educators 4 (2006).

41. Marian Murphy et.al., *Reflective Inquiry in Social Work Education*, in Handbook of Reflection and Reflective Inquiry: Mapping a Way of Knowing for Professional Reflective Inquiry 177 (2010).

42. P. J. Feltovich et. al, *Studies of Expertise from Psychological Perspectives*, in The Cambridge Handbook of Expertise and Expert Performance 55 (K. Anders Ericsson et. al. eds., 2006).

43. Just Write Guide, *41. [https://lincs.ed.gov/sites/default/files/TEAL_JustWriteGuide.pdf]

44. Anthony S. Niedwiecki, *Lawyers and Learning: A Metacognitive Approach to Legal Education*, 13 Widener L. Rev. 33, 42-43 (2006).

45. Just Write Guide, *supra* at *32.

46. This model is based on a model at About.com: Psychology. http://psychology.about.com/od/problemsolving/f/problem-solving-steps.htm.

47. Michael Hunter Schwartz, *Teaching Law Students to Be Self-Regulated Learners*, 2003 MICH ST. DCL L. REV. 447, 454.

Chapter Two
Optimism Biases

Chapter Goals.
1. To discuss the optimism biases in detail.
2. To give the reader ways to overcome the optimism biases.

In the next few chapters, I will group similar biases together and treat them in detail. This chapter will cover optimism biases: the optimism bias, confirmation bias, expectation bias, illusion of control, normalcy bias, overconfidence effect, planning fallacy, Semmelweis reflex, and subjective validation.

I. Optimism Bias

Let's start with the optimism bias since it partially encompasses the others in this section. Optimism bias: "The tendency to be over-optimistic, overestimating favorable and pleasing outcomes."[1] It is "a mismatch resulting from one's future expectations exceeding the reality of the outcome."[2] It is "the difference between a person's expectation and the outcome that follows. If expectations are better than reality, the bias is optimistic; if reality is better than expected, the bias is pessimistic."[3] It is not limited by race, gender, national origin, or age.[4] One writer has declared, "The optimism bias is pervasive, relatively stubborn and notoriously unwavering to contradiction."[5] Can you see how this bias is particularly problematic for lawyers? For one thing, it often interferes with reasonable compromises.

Under Kahneman's analysis, this bias occurs because individuals "place too much faith in their intuitions."[6] "If System 1 is involved, the conclusions come first and the [supporting] arguments follow,"[7] without much thought.

Examples.
Julia will go to the prom with me, even though she is the most popular girl in school.
I am sure to get the job even though there are lots of applicants.
I can jump the gap between the two high buildings.
If I complete college, I will get a good job and be able to support a family.
I don't need a stockbroker. I'm lucky at picking stocks. Or, I am better at picking stocks than the average investor.[8]
I know there is a lot of crime downtown, but I'll be okay going to that bar.
It's okay I'm a little drunk. I can drive home safely.
I know it's dangerous to drive and text, but I can do it.
The operation will be a success, even though the doctor told me that it has only a 10% chance of succeeding.
I know smoking is dangerous, but I won't get cancer.
I know I can get pregnant, but I am having sex just one time without a condom.
I don't need to buy renter's insurance. Nothing will happen to my stuff.
If I file a lawsuit, I will win.
My new business will be very successful. I am a better than the average manager.
It won't be a problem paying off my student debt.

My alma mater couldn't have cheated at basketball recruitment.
Physicians "who were 'completely certain' of the diagnosis antemortem were wrong 40% of the time."[9]

Legal Examples.
Overestimating the chances of winning a case.
Telling a client that he is certain to win his case.
Thinking that you have come up with the best argument on the first try.
Thinking that the contract you drafted will not lead to litigation.
Thinking that the judge has to accept your argument.
Thinking that you are the best lawyer to argue the case.

Optimists are lucky, and they provide many benefits to society.[10] They are happy, have less stress, take action, persist in the face of obstacles, and influence others. They drive the "engine of capitalism" because they are risk takers.

However, being overly-optimistic can cause great harm in your life because the optimism bias causes people to ignore risks.[11] Consider the example above on jumping between two buildings. What happens if you don't make it? Similar things can happen if you are too optimistic concerning your life plans. It is great to reach for the stars, but always have a back-up plan.

CEOs often exhibit the optimism bias. For example, a CEO may recommend the acquisition of a company because she thinks she can manage it better than the current managers.[12] Can you see the problems with this thought? Similarly, one writer thinks the optimism bias was responsible for the 2008 financial crisis.[13]

The optimism bias occurs because "[h]umans demonstrate selective attention toward incoming positive information concerning the future. Beliefs are then differentially updated in favour of this preferred positive information."[14] Humans simplify situations in their minds.[15] We overestimate positive events and discount negative ones.[16] Temporal distance can also affect how we view future events.[17] Finally, individuals "tend to be overly optimistic about their relative standing on any activity in which they do moderately well."[18] (A good pianist thinks she can be a concert pianist.)

In sum, "Excessive optimism is the result of a facile illusion we create for ourselves. In visualizing an uncomplicated future, we rise above the myriad of possible outcomes to focus on a simplified positive endpoint. Admittedly, to reconcile the full spectrum of conceivable eventualities would be endlessly time-consuming and tortuous. And it is as such, that the optimism bias exists as a heavily-biased heuristic to satiate our hunger for certainty– even if it is one of our own creation."[19]

Exercises II-1

1. Are you an optimist or a pessimist?
2. Think of times in your life when being overly-optimistic caused you problems.
3. Do any of your friends or relatives suffer from the optimism bias? How has it affected their lives?

4. What are the consequences of texting while driving? Have you heard of any accidents caused by texting? Did you know that experts think texting while driving is as dangerous as drunk driving?
5. Have you ever driven drunk? Did you get home safely? Was this due to your skill or your luck? Do you think you will be as lucky next time? (A girl I knew in high school was killed in a drunk driving accident during her senior year.) Do you owe a responsibility to others not to drive drunk? How would you feel if you killed someone while driving drunk? What would your parents say if they knew you had driven drunk? Would they be right?
6. Are you more or less likely than your friends to get cancer?
7. Are you more or less likely than your friends to be a victim of a crime?
8. Are you more or less likely than your friends to get married?
9. Are you more or less likely than your friends to become a success?
10. Do you think that you will have a higher starting salary than your friends who are in the same major?
11. Think up at least ten more instances in which lawyers might suffer from an optimism bias.
12. Can you see how an optimism bias might affect a lawyer's well-being?

Comment: Studies show the individuals are less likely to exhibit the optimism bias when they make comparisons.[20] Another way to overcome the optimism bias is through careful planning. Be your own "devil's advocate." Also, see the wrap up below.

Example.
Carrie thought that she could get a good job after law school. Despite her optimism, she did a great deal of research on law school careers. This research showed that her optimism was wrong. With her college grades and LSAT score, she was unlikely to get a good job if she went to law school.

    To avoid being overly-optimistic with a client, thoroughly analyze the law and facts of the case. Then, come up with the otherside's best arguments. Only after these steps, give your client an analysis of her chances. You also need to recognize that your client could be suffering from the optimism bias. This should affect how you communicate with your client. Don't let her leave your office with a mistaken impression of her chances, or you will have problems if the case doesn't go well.
    Please note that having these optimism biases is not necessarily bad. Some scientists believe that the optimism biases are an adaptive feature that causes individuals to continue to persevere, rather than giving up.[21] Just be careful to use your System 2 to evaluate your System 1 biases. Ask why am I optimistic? Is my optimism consistent with reality?
    Now, let's consider some specific optimism biases.

II. Confirmation Bias

    A confirmation bias is "[t]he tendency to search for, interpret, focus on and remember information in a way that confirms one's preconceptions."[22] In other words, it's wishful thinking (not objective thinking); the brain is unconsciously trying to confirm an individual's beliefs. These biases affect the gathering of information, interpretation of information, and recall of information.[23] Such biases can be very harmful when they affect policy planning, medical diagnoses, and legal advice.

As one writer has noted, "There is an obvious difference between impartially evaluating evidence in order to come to an unbiased conclusion and building a case to justify a conclusion already drawn. In the first instance one seeks evidence on all sides of a question, evaluates it as objectively as one can, and draws the conclusion that the evidence, in the aggregate, seems to dictate. In the second, one selectively gathers, or gives undue weight to, evidence that supports one's position while neglecting to gather, or discounting, evidence that would tell against it."[24] Stated differently, a confirmation bias is unconscious case-building.[25]

Confirmation biases can be motivated or unmotivated.[26] Biases based on emotion can be especially harmful. Another factor affecting this bias is that data found early in the research process will carry more weight than later information (the primacy effect).[27] Another part of the confirmation bias is the "own judgment evaluation" in which individuals overstate the confidence they have in their own judgments.[28]

Kahneman believes that "[t]he confirmatory bias of System I favors uncritical acceptance of suggestions and exaggeration of the likelihood of extreme and improbable events,"[29] System 1 "is biased to believe and confirm," and it "neglects ambiguity and suppresses doubt."[30]

Other causes.
The inability to handle complex tasks.
Use of heuristics, like the availability heuristic (how readily an idea comes to mind).
The difficulty of dealing with more than one heuristic at a time.
Overlooking challenges to existing beliefs.
Wishful thinking (emotional effect).
Preferring pleasant outcomes to painful ones.
Trying to avoid costly errors.[31]
People want to justify their own views.[32]

Examples.
Clinton will win the election because these polls show her ahead. The polls showing that Trump is gaining ground are outliers.
I believe that red heads are smarter than other people. All the good evidence supports this.
Congress should not control guns. I can name two incidents where the presence of guns saved lives. The mass shootings were not caused by guns, they were caused by the mentally ill. We need to treat the mentally ill, not ban guns.
Congress should control guns. The recent shooting at Fisherville by a mentally ill man proves this. It may be true he had an illegally-purchased gun, but we must keep guns out of the hands of the mentally ill.
The universe revolves around the earth. The bending of the horizon is merely an optical illusion.
ObamaCare has worked well because it has gotten more people health insurance. Higher premiums and the effects on state budgets are just minor problems that will disappear with

Optimism Biases

time.

Legal Examples.
After you have analyzed a case, discounting all evidence that contradicts your conclusion.
As a prosecutor, you need to be especially careful. If you think that the defendant is guilty, don't focus just on the evidence that supports that. As stated above, try to look at all problems from several angles.
A lawyer advises a client not to settle a case because she is sure that she will win at trial despite conflicting evidence.
A confirmation bias may affect how a lawyer handles a case. In other words, the lawyer may not attack contradictory evidence because he thinks it isn't important.

Overcoming a Confirmation Bias

1. Awareness of the possibility of this bias. Don't cling to your theory. It is okay to make mistakes.
2. Weigh all evidence equally, regardless of when you obtained it. (Primacy effect)
3. Slow down. System 1 is fast; System 2 is slow.
4. Is the outcome the same as what you believed at the beginning? If so, check your reasoning and reevaluate the facts.
5. Evaluation and self-monitoring. Always check your thinking process to see if it is based on a confirmation bias or on careful, objective thinking. Examine each step of the process: information gathering, interpretation, recall. Have you considered all reasonable hypotheses? Always consider all sides of an argument or problem.
6. Consider your view to be a hypothesis. Just like any other hypothesis you have to prove it, and you need to account for negative evidence.
7. Did you desire the outcome? Is it more pleasant than the alternatives? Has the idea that one of the outcomes might be painful affected your reasoning?
8. Try to look at the problem from someone else's viewpoint. What would my professor (or boss) say about my decision-making process?

Above all, acknowledge your ignorance–lack of knowledge. Nobody knows everything. There is no shame in not knowing something. The shame is in refusing to acknowledge your ignorance and, consequently, making mistakes. If you acknowledge your ignorance, you can then seek the knowledge you need to solve a problem.

Exercises II-2

1. Think of times you might have been affected by a confirmation bias. Were you wrong? What effect did the confirmation bias have? What would you have done differently if you had been aware of the confirmation bias?
2. Have you observed confirmation biases in others–relatives, friends, bosses, co-workers, teachers, cable news shows? Were they right or wrong? How did the confirmation bias affect those people?

3. Write down all the ways you can overcome your confirmation biases?
4. Do you do the things listed above to avoid confirmation biases? Are you willing to include them in your thinking routine?
5. Do you generally self-monitor and evaluate your thinking? If you don't, you should develop these habits.
6. Do you always consider all sides of an argument or problem? If not, you should develop this habit. What will my opponent (the defendant) argue in this case? What will my political opponent argue? What will my debate opponent argue?
5. Most people have a strong opinion on gun control. Has the confirmation bias affected your opinion on gun control? Write down all the arguments of the otherside on gun control? From an objective viewpoint are these arguments reasonable?
6. What is your opinion on same-sex marriage? Write down all the arguments that support your position. Write down all the arguments that support the opposing position. Which side has the best position objectively?
7. Do the same as 6 for several different controversial topics. Does your side always win? If so, you are probably suffering from the confirmation bias.
8. Has a confirmation bias ever affected how you handled a case? How? What was the outcome?

III. Expectation Bias

The expectation bias is "[t]he tendency for experimenters to believe, certify, and publish data that agree with their expectations for the outcome of an experiment, and to disbelieve, discard, or downgrade the corresponding weightings for data that appear to conflict with those expectations."[33] I hope you can see how this is similar to the confirmation bias.

Examples.
When the outcome of the experiment doesn't come out the way you expected, you think you made a mistake.
My experiment will prove that the universe revolves around the Earth.
We must imprison that Galileo guy. He is trying to prove that the Earth revolves around the Sun.
He hit thirty home runs last season; he will hit thirty home runs this season.
The stock market did very well this year. I should invest because it will do well next year.
Failing a test and blaming the teacher for writing a bad test.
Her brother did well in my class, so she is smart, too.
I'll serve fried chicken when he comes. (He is from Kentucky. He'll love it.)
The waiter was slow in taking our order. He's going to ruin the entire meal.
When Marge thinks that Bart broke the lamp because he is always breaking things, when Lisa, the good one, really did it.
All the waiters are nasty on Neptune.
I can text while I drive. The other drivers will watch out for me.
My relationship with Mike will be better than my one with Jorge.
Have you noticed that experienced players get more of the benefit of the doubt than rookies on

Optimism Biases

close calls in baseball?

This is from an episode of *All in the Family*. A father and a son are in a horrible traffic accident. The father is killed, and the boy is rushed into surgery. When the surgeon sees the boy, the surgeon shouts, "I can't operate, this is my son." Explain: The usual explanation is that the surgeon is the boy's step-father. However, the answer is that the surgeon is his mother. If you got this one wrong, you had the expectation that surgeons are men. This was very common in the 70s when *All in the Family* aired, but today many surgeons are women. In any case, this is an example of an expectation bias.

Legal Examples.
Being stunned when you lose a case.
When a case doesn't come out your way, you blame someone else, such as the judge, an associate, or an opposing attorney's dishonesty.
Being stunned when a will you wrote is contested.
A law professor writing a journal article that discounts all evidence that opposes her theory.
Not listening to the other lawyers on your case.
Being surprised by a judge's ruling on the admissibility of evidence.

Overcoming an Expectation Bias

1. Make sure you have all the evidence before you start the analysis. Don't jump to conclusions based on incomplete evidence. Be able to explain your reasoning process.
2. Expectations are fine, but don't discount data that disagrees with your expectation. Actively seek contrary data. Make this part of your decision-making protocol.
3. Avoid framing biases. (see Chapter Five)
4. Be critical of your analytical method.
5. Account for (explain) all negative evidence.
6. Be flexible in your thinking. Don't let unexpected outcomes rattle you.
7. Avoid stereotyping. Realize that a stereotype doesn't always apply to a member of a group. Stereotypes are generalizations that omit relevant details.
8. Consult with others.
9. Test and retest when possible. (In other words, double-check your work.)

Another way to overcome this bias is to weigh the evidence and other support critically. For example, say six studies conclude X, and only one study concludes Y. The Y study could still be the best support for a conclusion if it is the most recent study. Same example. The Y study could be the best support for a conclusion if it was done by a leader in the field, while the X studies were all done by high school students. Same example. The Y study could be the best study to support a conclusion if it is the most thorough study, while the X studies are superficial.

Exercises II-3

1. Think of instances in which you suffered from an expectation bias. What mistakes did you

make? How did it affect you?
2. Imagine you are driving to work or school or the mall. Try to visualize all the expectation biases you might have while driving.
3. Imagine you are flying an airplane. What are the possible expectation biases?
4. Think of how stereotyping caused you to come to the wrong conclusion.
5. Think how an expectation bias affected you in your law practice.

IV. Illusion of Control

Illusion of control is "the tendency to overestimate one's degree of influence over other external events."[34] Another side to this bias is that people think they have control over chance events. It is caused by "priority - the thought occurred before the action; consistency - the thought is consistent with the action; and exclusivity - no other potential causes are present."[35]

Examples.
I can make golfers on tv miss putts.
The Mets lost because I didn't wear my lucky hat.
I am very good at picking winners at the race track.
I won't get into a traffic accident because I am a safe driver.
Affecting someone by sticking pins in a voodoo doll.
I can make this project succeed.

Legal Examples.
Thinking you will win a case when you haven't seen your opponent's brief. (You can't control your opponent's arguments or the judge's thinking process.)
Thinking you will win a negotiation because you are a great negotiator. (Not only might you not be as good as your think, your opponent might be a great negotiator, too. Or, the otherside had the best argument to begin with.)

Overcoming the Illusion of Control

1. Examine how much control you really have over the situation. Develop introspective insight as to whether you control a situation.
2. Ask what is outside your control.
3. Accept the fact that sometimes there may be nothing you can do.
4. Consider the consequences of this bias in particular situations. (What are the consequences if I am wrong that I can text and drive at the same time?)

Exercises II-4

1. Think of times in your life when you suffered from the illusion of control. How did this affect the outcome? Did it cause any problems? Have you ever committed to a risky plan of action because you thought you had control over the situation?
2. Have you seen the illusion of control in others? How did it affect their ability to make

sound judgments?
3. Have you seen the illusion of control in public figures?
4. You are in a gambling casino. How might the illusion of control affect you? Can you compensate for the illusion of control?
5. Do the same exercise with the stock market.
6. Are you a perfectionist? Do you blame yourself for things that are not your fault? (The project failed. I controlled the project. The project's failure was really my fault. Of course, sometimes it really is your fault, but carefully evaluate the situation before you blame yourself.)
7. Do you try to control your environment? Do you try to control others? Can you control everything in your life?
8. Do you see how the illusion of control can affect settlements?
9. Can you see how the illusion of control affects how you work with others?
10. Can you see how the illusion of control might affect an attorney's well-being?

V. The Normalcy Bias

Normalcy bias: "The refusal to plan for, or react to, a disaster which has never happened before."[36] Also called analysis paralysis, the ostrich effect, or the black swan. The ostrich effect is hiding your head in the sand. The black swan is based on the fact that Europeans had never seen a black swan before. When they were told they existed in Australia, they had trouble believing they existed. For example, I told my students that the financial crash of 2008 was a black swan. The experts had never experienced an economic event like 2008 before so they were not prepared when it happened.

Because it prevents disaster planning, the normalcy bias can have disastrous effects. Morever, because it is an optimism bias, it can cause people to ignore warnings.

"The normalcy bias may be caused in part by the way the brain processes new data. Research suggests that even when the brain is calm, it takes 8–10 seconds to process new information. Stress slows the process, and when the brain cannot find an acceptable response to a situation, it fixates on a single and sometimes default solution that may or may not be correct. An evolutionary reason for this response could be that paralysis gives an animal a better chance of surviving an attack; predators are less likely to see prey that is not moving."[37]

Examples.
The island didn't have enough food or water when the hurricane hit.
The company lacked the cash reserves to survive the recession.
The townspeople stared at the power of the mighty volcano, causing many of them to flee too late and perish.
Marcia only applied to one college. When she didn't get into that college, she thought her life was over.
The attack at Pearl Harbor.
The fall of the Soviet Union.
A young father dying without any insurance to support his family.
The fact that the Earth is round to pre-Columbians.

Understanding and Overcoming Cognitive Biases for Lawyers and Law Students

Legal Examples.
Being blind-sided when the other side comes up with a novel argument.
Not being prepared when a client acts out-of-character.
Not making novel arguments yourself.
Always relying on the default solution.

I once read a story about how a member of the Swedish royal family found an Indonesian man on a bench outside the royal palace who was freezing to death because he was only lightly dressed. He hadn't experienced cold before. The prince gave the man his coat and had his guard take the man into the warmth of the palace. The man recovered.

This story might be an urban legend, but it is an extreme example of a normalcy bias. The man had never experienced cold before so he didn't know what effect it would have on him.

Of course, examples of the ostrich effect can be less vivid than those above. Ignoring negative business data is a good example. Ignoring negative business data is common, and it can lead to losses and even bankruptcy.

Overcoming the Normalcy Bias

1. Try to see alternative possibilities.
2. Get more information (if there is time). Don't ignore negative information.
3. Consider both the possibility and severity of an event. Create a mental picture of the event, including details.
4. Visualize possible outcomes.
5. Don't delay planning.
6. Try to remain calm in stressful situations.

Exercises II-5

1. Have you ever felt the black swan effect–when something happened that you didn't think was possible? How did you react? How could you have prevented the normalcy bias in this case?
2. Think up some black swans in history? How could they have been prevented?
3. Have there been any black swans in recent public life? How could they have been prevented?
4. Can you see how the normalcy bias impedes creativity?
5. Think up more common examples of the ostrich effect.
6. Do you overly-rely on the normalcy bias in your practice?
7. Have you ever been blind sided in your practice.

VI. Overconfidence Effect

The overconfidence effect is "[e]xcessive confidence in one's own answers to

Optimism Biases

questions."[38] This bias involves both overestimation ("the tendency to overestimate one's standing on a dimension of judgment or performance") and over-precision ("the excessive confidence that one knows the truth").[39] There are three types of the overconfidence bias: "(1) overestimation of one's actual performance, (2) over-placement of one's performance relative to others, and (3) excessive precision in one's beliefs."[40] The illusion of control and the planning fallacy can contribute to the overconfidence bias.[41] This one is obviously similar to the optimism bias.

Examples.
The merger will help both companies.
Our nation will quickly defeat Elbonia in the war.
I will easily win Wisconsin so I don't have to campaign there.
I will make a lot of money by flipping houses.
Our union will win the strike quickly.
I know law school is hard, but I'm sure I'll graduate in the top 10% of my class.
I am a better driver than any of my friends.
It is okay if I text while I drive because I am a good driver.

Legal Examples.
We are certain to win this case.
This is the best possible contract for your situation.
There will be no problems with the merger.
The case will settle in our favor.
The contract will be signed in two weeks.

CEOs often believe that they are responsible for the success of their companies. Kahneman suggests that the correlation between the CEO and the success of a company is about .30.[42] He adds, "A correlation of .30 implies that you would find the stronger CEO leading the stronger firm in 60% of the pairs–an improvement of a mere 10 percentage points over random guessing, hardly grist for the hero worship of CEOs we often witness." Think about coaches that are successful with one team then not with another. Has the coach gotten worse? Has there been a regression to the mean? Was the coach's success due to luck or lack of luck? Was it due to the quality of the players?

Obviously the overconfidence bias can have disastrous consequences. It causes individuals to take too much risk and planners to stop planning too early.

Overcoming the Overconfidence Bias

1. Always consider the possible presence of this bias in your thinking.
2. Make sure you have all the facts.
3. Consider alternatives.
4. Confer with others.
5. Consider the consequences of being overconfident.
6. It is okay to make mistakes.

7. Make a list of your strengths and weaknesses.
8. Us accountability mechanisms.

Exercises II-6

1. Read an account of the explosion of the space shuttle Challenger. How did overconfidence contribute to this accident?
2. Think of times where the overconfidence effect affected your thinking. What were the consequences? What could you have done to overcome the effect in those cases?
3. Think of times where the overconfidence effect has influenced others? What were the consequences in those cases?
4. Think of instances of the overconfidence effect in history. What were the consequences?
5. Can the overconfidence effect cause you to be resentful of the successes of others? Do you blame others for your failures because of the overconfidence effect? (Ex. I failed the exam because my teacher did a poor job in writing it.)
6. Quickly write down several things you do better than your friends. Now critically evaluate the list. Was the overconfidence effect operating with any of these items?
7. Reflect on how the illusion of control affects the confidence bias.
8. Does the fact that a business succeeded mean that other companies should hire its CEO or adopt its business model?
9. Think of a successful television show or movie franchise? How often have other producers imitated those shows or movies and succeeded?
10. Think how the overconfidence bias has affected you in practice. I bet it has affected you a lot because successful people often suffer from this bias.

In sum, "errors of prediction are inevitable because the world is unpredictable."[43] There is much more randomness in our lives than we think. As Kahneman has noted, "It is wise to take admissions of uncertainty seriously, but declarations of high confidence mainly tell you that an individual has constructed a coherent story in his mind, not necessarily that the story is true."[44]

VII. Planning Fallacy

The planning fallacy, a type of the optimism bias, concerns decisions and forecasts in policy, planning, and management, such as the underestimating costs of a project or the overestimating the benefits.[45] It is often the main cause of overspending on projects.[46]

Examples.
I can write this paper tonight.
I can complete this project in a week even though similar projects have taken me three weeks.
No one can understand why the construction of the museum took twice as long as estimated.
Any Defense Department project.

Legal Examples.

Optimism Biases

I can write this brief over the weekend.
I don't understand how we lost the case; we had a great strategy.
I don't understand why the contract negotiations failed.
I don't understand why my client's corporation failed; we came up with a great business plan.

Scientists have theorized the following causes for this bias:
1. Planners focus on the most optimistic scenario.[47]
2. Wishful thinking.
3. The self-serving bias.
4. Focalism–focusing on the future rather than the past.
5. Recall failure.
6. Temporal frames.[48]

Overcoming the Planning Fallacy

1. Determine how much time similar projects have taken (or cost) in the past.
2. Estimate the time for subtasks and add them up.
3. Get multiple estimates from unconnected sources.
4. Consider the consequences of the planning fallacy. (What will happen if the project is finished late? What will happen if there are cost overruns?)
5. Be your group's "devil's advocate."

Like many of the optimism biases, the planning fallacy can have positive effects. The planning fallacy can cause a company to take on a project it would not have taken on if it had know how long it would actually take or how much it would actually cost.[49] Once the project is started, the company is forced to continue it. Thus, difficult projects are completed in cases they might not have been.

Exercises II-7

1. When you plan a project, do you consider how much time similar projects have taken in the past?
2. When you planned for a vacation, did you estimate the cost correctly?
3. When you were in college, did you estimate the time to write a paper accurately?
4. What problems has the planning fallacy caused you?
5. Think of several ways the planning fallacy can hurt a business.
6. Think of several times the planning fallacy has had a beneficial effect.
7. Do your legal projects usually finish within your time estimate?
8. Do your lawsuits always come in under estimated costs?
9. Think of an instance where your litigation strategy failed. Why did it fail?
10. Think of a time when a tax strategy failed. Why did it fail?
11. Think of a time when a business plan failed. Why did it fail.

VIII. Semmelweis Reflex

Understanding and Overcoming Cognitive Biases for Lawyers and Law Students

Semmelweis reflex: "The tendency to reject new evidence that contradicts a paradigm."[50] In other words, people instinctively fear the new. Don't we do this one all the time? Can you see how this relates to the expectation bias? It is the expectation bias from a new angle.

Semmelweis was concerned with the high infant mortality rate at a hospital.[51] He had observed that doctors had gone directly from the autopsy lab to the maternity ward. He proposed that doctors wash their hands before handling babies. Other doctors ridiculed his proposal because gentlemen don't need to wash their hands. Babies continued to die at high rates until doctors started washing their hands many years later.

Examples.
I've always smoked cigarettes, and they haven't made me sick. The new studies showing cigarettes can cause cancer are nonsense.
We don't need to change the way we educate law students. The studies that purport to show that there are better ways are not reliable.
I know there are studies that show that vaccines don't cause autism, but I know they are wrong.
That candidate can't possibly support affirmative action even though he says he does. All conservatives are against affirmative action.
Darwin was wrong because evolution doesn't agree with the Bible.
I understand that studies have proven genetically-engineered food is safe. I'm still not going to eat it.
That Galileo guy should be put to death. The Earth doesn't revolve around the Sun.
I know that no scientific study supports the healing power of crystals. I just know they work.

Legal Examples.
Ignoring evidence that contradicts your strategy in litigation. Can you see what problems this one might cause?
Ignoring evidence that your client is guilty. If your client is guilty, it isn often better for the client if you plea bargain rather than go to trial.

Scott Adams once published a Dilbert book entitled "Since When Did Ignorance Become a Point of View."

Causes.
1. Putting more faith in theories than facts and observations.
2. Over-reliance on common sense.
3. The effect of emotions on reasoning.

Overcoming the Semmelweis Reflex

1. Don't automatically reject an idea because it is new or because it conflicts with long-held beliefs.
2. Use common sense and a reliable problem-solving method, rather than just relying on common sense.

Optimism Biases

3. Consider how the history of science is based on disproving well-established theories.
4. Carefully examine the basis of new versus existing theories. Which one has more factual support? Be data driven.
5. What are the consequences if the new evidence is correct?

Exercises II-8

1. Think of times you have suffered from the Semmelweis reflex? Why did you reject the new evidence or theory?
2. Think of more examples of this bias. What were the results of these examples?
3. How does this reflex affect the acquisition of knowledge? How might it affect your education?
4. Has this bias ever negatively affected how you litigated a case?
5. Have you ever given a client bad advice because of this bias?

IX. Subjective Validation

Subjective validation: "Perception that something is true if a subject's belief demands it to be true. Also assigns perceived connections between coincidences."[52] It is also "called the 'personal validation effect' because it refers to a process by which people accept some claim or phenomenon as valid based solely upon a few personal experiences and/or subjective perception."[53] Also called the Barnum effect (gullibility)–"The Barnum Effect is a product of people's predilection to believe positive statements about themselves, even when there is no particular reason to do so."[54] Can you see how this bias related to the other optimism biases?

Examples.
An astrology reading that confirms an individual's ideas about himself.
(With astrology readings, the person remembers what is right about herself, but forgets the wrong items.)
A teacher telling a student that he or she is an excellent student when the teacher actually knows little about the student.
Saying that an artist has done an excellent job with a portrait when the portrait makes us look better than we are.
Believing that a psychic can contact the dead.

Legal Example.
A poor lawyer's advice confirms to a client that he should plead not guilty.
Feeling that you have to go beyond ethical limits because there is no other way to convince a jury that your client is not guilty.

Overcoming Subjective Validation

1. Doing an independent evaluation.
2. Is my conclusion based on the evidence or my opinion of the other person? Be data driven.

Understanding and Overcoming Cognitive Biases for Lawyers and Law Students

Exercises II-9

1. Have you ever suffered from subjective validation?
2. Have you seen this bias in others?
3. Think about how subjective validation works with the Semmelweis reflex.
4. Has this bias ever affected how you tried a case?
5. Has this bias ever lead to you doing an unethical act?

Wrap Up

Overcoming Optimism Biases

1. Be aware that cognitive biases can affect your thinking.
2. Know the possible cognitive biases for a problem.
3. Have a consistent problem-solving strategy.
4. Be able to separate the objective from the subjective.
5. Slow down. Make sure you have all the evidence and that you have considered all alternatives. Account for all the negative evidence.
6. Evaluation and self-monitoring.
7. Avoid wishful thinking. Ask whether you desired the outcome. If so, recheck your reasoning process.
8. Be critical of your analytical method. Try to criticize your method as if you were someone else.
9. Consider alternatives.
10. Consult with others.
11. Try to keep your emotions separate from the reasoning process.
12. Consider the risks of making a mistake.
13. Be able to explain your reasoning process.

Getting all the evidence and considering all alternatives is particularly important in overcoming biases. Consider a murder trial. The decision-making will be very different if only the prosecution presents evidence, instead of having both sides present evidence. The same is true with your reasoning; to make a proper decision; you must consider all sides.

Exercises II-10

Identify the possible cognitive biases.

1. Although there are several contradictory studies, the best one supports my theory.
2. The project will succeed because I am in charge of the group.
3. I know I will get the job because my psychic said I would.
4. The project will cost $1,000,000.
5. Self-driving cars are ridiculous. A car needs a human driving it.
6. The union will return to work quickly when their emergency fund is depleted.

Optimism Biases

7. Seven other studies support my conclusion. (The researcher has failed to mention five studies that disagree.)
8. I am sure I will get the best grade on the exam.
9. I am sure I will be a great doctor even though I didn't do so well with science in college.
10. If I concentrate hard enough, I can make my favorite player hit a home run.
11. We can easily complete construction in two years.
12. All Martians are rude.
13. I know that my doctor said to get more exercise, but I feel good.
14. The studies that say cell phones can cause cancer are wrong. We should throw those researchers in jail.
15. This area can't be hit by an earthquake because one has not hit before.
16. We are certain to win the case.
17. It will take two weeks to negotiate the contract.
18. The new witness must be lying. All the other evidence demonstrates that the defendant is guilty.
19. The otherside will not make that argument. It is too novel for the judge to accept.
20. I am meeting with the other attorney tomorrow. I will get him to make all the concessions you want.
21. Yes, your honor. We won't have any problem meeting the deadlines in the discovery agreement.
22. My client cannot be guilty. Therefore, it is okay to let the witness lie about his alibi.
23. Subjective validation.

Answers

Your answers may differ from mine because the biases overlap. However, you should be able to back up your answer.

1. Confirmation bias. Ask why you think it is the best study–because it is objectively the best study or because it supports your theory?
2. Illusion of control.
3. Subjective validation.
4. Possible planning fallacy.
5. Semmelweis reflex.
6. Overconfidence effect.
7. Expectation bias.
8. Optimism bias or overconfidence effect.
9. Overconfidence effect.
10. Illusion of control.
11. Possible planning fallacy.
12. Expectation bias.
13. Optimism bias.
14. Semmelweis reflex.
15. Normalcy bias.

16. Optimism bias or overconfidence effect.
17. Planning fallacy.
18. Expectation bias or Semmelweis reflex.
19. Normalcy bias.
20. Illusion of control.
21. Planning fallacy.

Now that you have examined several cognitive biases in detail, have you become more aware of the cognitive biases in your thinking? Awareness is the key to fighting cognitive biases and developing clear thinking.

Notes

1. *Wikipedia: List of Cognitive Biases.* [https://en.wikipedia.org/wiki/List_of_cognitive_biases]

2. Owen P. O'Sullivan, *The Neural Basis of Always Looking on the Bright Side*, 8 Dial Phil Ment Neuro Sci 11, 12 (2015). [http://www.crossingdialogues.com/Ms-A14-09.pdf]

3. Tali Sharot, *The Optimism Bias*, 21 Current Biology 941 (2011). [http://www.sciencedirect.com/science/article/pii/S0960982211011912]

4. O'Sullivan, *supra* at 12.

5. *Id.* at 12-13.

6. Daniel Kahneman, Thinking, Fast and Slow 45 (2011).

7. *Id.*.

8. A study showed that "financial officers of large corporations had no clue about the short-term future of the stock market; the correlation between their estimates and the true value was slightly less than zero." *Id.* at 261.

9. *Id.* at 263.

10. *Id.* at 259; Shelley E. Taylor & Jonathon D. Brown, *Illusion and well-being: A social psychological perspective on mental health*, 103 Psychological Bulletin 193 (1988). [https://dx.doi.org/10.1037%2F0033-2909.103.2.193]

11. Neil D. Weinstein & William M. Klein, *Unrealistic Optimism: Present and Future*, 15 Journal of Social Change and Clinical Psychology 1, 1 (1996). [http://guilfordjournals.com/doi/abs/10.1521/jscp.1996.15.1.1] *See also* Kahneman, *supra* at 256-59.

12. Kahneman, *supra* at 258.

13. Sharot, *supra*.

14. O'Sullivan, *supra* at 13. The optimism bias is affected by dopamine in the brain. Some scientists believe that the optimism bias can be treated with L-DOPA. *Id.* at 13. However, one of the purposes of this book is to help you overcome your cognitive biases without therapy ort drugs.

15. *Id.* at 11.

16. *Id.* at 11-12.

17. *Id.* at 12.

18. Kahneman, *supra* at 260.

19. O'Sullivan, *supra* at 14.

20. Marie Helweg-Larsen & James A. Shepperd. *Do Moderators of the Optimistic Bias Affect Personal or Target Risk Estimates? A Review of the Literature*, 5 Personality and Social Psychology Review 74. [https://dx.doi.org/10.1207%2FS15327957PSPR0501_5]

21. Shelley E. Taylor & Jonathon D. Brown,(1988), *Illusion and well-being: A social psychological perspective on mental health*, 103 Psychological Bulletin 193 (1988). [https://dx.doi.org/10.1037%2F0033-2909.103.2.193]

22. Wikipedia: Cognitive Bias Mitigation, https://en.wikipedia.org/wiki/Cognitive_bias_mitigation.

23. Kendra Cherry, *What is a Confirmation Bias? Examples and Observations*, Verywell (June 22, 2016). [https://www.verywell.com/what-is-a-confirmation-bias-2795024]

24. Raymond S. Nickerson, *Confirmation Bias: A Ubiquitous Phenomenon in Many Guises*, 2 Review of General Psychology 175, 175 (1998). [http://landman-psychology.com/ConfirmationBias.pdf]

25. *Id.*

26. *Id.* at 176.

27. *Id.* at 187.

28. *Id.* at 188.

29. Kahneman, *supra* at 81.

30. *Id.* at 105.

31. *Wikipedia: Confirmation Bias.* [https://en.wikipedia.org/wiki/Confirmation_bias]

32. Hugo Mercier & Dan Sperber, *Why do humans reason? Arguments for an argumentative theory*, 34 Behavioral & Brain Sciences 57 (2011). [http://ssrn.com/abstract=1698090]

33. *Wikipedia: List of Cognitive Biases.*

34. *Id.*

35. Christin N. Hobbs et.al., *The illusion of control in a virtual reality setting*, 12 North American Journal of Psychology 1527 (2010). [http://www.freepatentsonline.com/article/North-American-Journal-Psychology/245167898.html]

36. *Wikipedia: List of Cognitive Biases.*

37. *Wikipedia: Normalcy Bias.* [https://en.wikipedia.org/wiki/Normalcy_bias]

38. *Wikipedia: List of Cognitive Biases.*

39. *Wikipedia: Overconfidence Effect.* [https://en.wikipedia.org/wiki/Overconfidence_effect]

40. Don A. Moore & Paul J. Healy, *The Trouble with Ovberconfidence*, (2007). [http://repository.cmu.edu/cgi/viewcontent.cgi?article=1340&context=tepper]

41. *Id.*

42. Kahneman, *supra* at 205.

43. *Id.* at 220.

44. *Id.* at 212.

45. *Wikipedia: Optimism Bias.* [https://en.wikipedia.org/wiki/Optimism_bias]

46. Bent Flyvbjerg, *Over Budget, Over Time, Over and Over Again: Managing Major Projects*, in Peter W. G. Morris et.al. The Oxford Handbook of Project Management. 321 (2011). [https://dx.doi.org/10.1093%2Foxfordhb%2F9780199563142.003.0014]

47. Kahneman, *supra* at 255.

48. *Wikipedia: Planning Fallacy.* [https://en.wikipedia.org/wiki/Planning_fallacy]

49. Albert O. Hirschman, *The Principle of the Hiding Hand.* [http://www.nationalaffairs.com/doclib/20080516_196700602theprincipleofthehidinghandalbertohirschman.pdf]

50. *Wikipedia: List of Cognitive Biases.*

51. Esther Inglis-Arkell, *The Semmelweis Reflex explains why people reject the new*, io9 (2013). [http://io9.gizmodo.com/the-semmelweis-reflex-explains-why-people-reject-the-ne-1451234126]
Some scientiosts have rejected the Semmelwies narrative as an urban myth. However, it remains an excellent example of the bias.

52. *Wikipedia: List of Cognitive Biases.*

53. Austin Cline, *Flaws in Reasoning and Arguments: Subjective Validation*, [http://atheism.about.com/od/logicalflawsinreasoning/a/subjective.htm]

54. *Id..*

Chapter Three
Negativity Biases

<u>Chapter Goals</u>.
1. To discuss the negativity biases in detail.
2. To give the reader ways to overcome the negativity biases.
3. To introduce the reader to mindfulness and well-being.
4. To introduce the reader to the growth mindset..

I. Negativity Biases

A. Introduction to Negativity Biases

Negativity biases exist because the human brain tends to focus on the negative.[1] "When making judgments, people consistently weight the negative aspects of an event or stimulus more heavily than the positive aspects."[2] This is because the human brain evolved to prioritize dangerous situations as a survival mechanism.[3]

Professors Lukianoff and Haidt have created an excellent list of common negativity biases:[4]

1. Mind reading. You assume that you know what people think without having sufficient evidence of their thoughts. "He thinks I'm a loser."
2. Fortune-telling. You predict the future negatively: things will get worse, or there is danger ahead. "I'll fail that exam," or "I won't get the job."
3. Catastrophizing. You believe that what has happened or will happen will be so awful and unbearable that you won't be able to stand it. "It would be terrible if I failed."
4. Labeling. You assign global negative traits to yourself and others. "I'm undesirable," or "He's a rotten person."
5. Discounting positives. You claim that the positive things you or others do are trivial. "That's what wives are supposed to do—so it doesn't count when she's nice to me," or "Those successes were easy, so they don't matter."
6. Negative filtering. You focus almost exclusively on the negatives and seldom notice the positives. "Look at all of the people who don't like me."
7. Overgeneralizing. You perceive a global pattern of negatives on the basis of a single incident. "This generally happens to me. I seem to fail at a lot of things."
8. Dichotomous thinking. You view events or people in all-or-nothing terms. "I get rejected by everyone," or "It was a complete waste of time."
9. Blaming. You focus on the other person as the source of your negative feelings, and you refuse to take responsibility for changing yourself. "She's to blame for the way I feel now," or "My parents caused all my problems."
10. What if? You keep asking a series of questions about "what if" something happens, and you fail to be satisfied with any of the answers. "Yeah, but what if I get anxious?," or "What if I can't catch my breath?"

11. Emotional reasoning. You let your feelings guide your interpretation of reality. "I feel depressed; therefore, my marriage is not working out."

12. Inability to disconfirm. You reject any evidence or arguments that might contradict your negative thoughts. For example, when you have the thought I'm unlovable, you reject as irrelevant any evidence that people like you. Consequently, your thought cannot be refuted. "That's not the real issue. There are deeper problems. There are other factors."

Professors Lukianoff and Haidt declared, "For millennia, philosophers have understood that we don't see life as it is; we see a version distorted by our hopes, fears, and other attachments. The Buddha said, 'Our life is the creation of our mind.' Marcus Aurelius said, 'Life itself is but what you deem it.' The quest for wisdom in many traditions begins with this insight. Early Buddhists and the Stoics, for example, developed practices for reducing attachments, thinking more clearly, and finding release from the emotional torments of normal mental life."[5]

Negativity biases are an evolutionary product; they developed because fear kept our ancestors alive.[6] Consequently, humans "generally react[] more intensely to negative stimuli than to equally strong positive ones."[7] More specifically, negativity biases routinely trick brains into making three mistakes: "overestimating threats, underestimating opportunities, and underestimating resources (for dealing with threats and fulfilling opportunities)."[8] The result of this is partially physiological: two thirds of the neurons in the amygdala look for bad news.[9] The brain even reacts quickly to symbolic threats, such as emotionally-loaded words.[10]

With negativity biases, people allow emotions to control their thinking.[11] Professor Burns "defines emotional reasoning as assuming 'that your negative emotions necessarily reflect the way things really are: 'I feel it, therefore it must be true.'"[12] For example, "Emotional reasoning dominates many campus debates and discussions. A claim that someone's words are 'offensive' is not just an expression of one's own subjective feeling of offendedness. It is, rather, a public charge that the speaker has done something objectively wrong. It is a demand that the speaker apologize or be punished by some authority for committing an offense."[13]

Do negativity biases come from System 1 or System 2?

Professors Lukianoff and Haidt advocate "cognitive behavioral therapy to overcome our brain biases. They note that "It is the most extensively studied nonpharmaceutical treatment of mental illness, and is used widely to treat depression, anxiety disorders, eating disorders, and addiction." They add that "Unlike drugs, cognitive behavioral therapy keeps working long after treatment is stopped, because it teaches thinking skills that people can continue to use."

The goal of cognitive behavioral therapy "is to minimize distorted thinking and see the world more accurately. You start by learning the names of the dozen or so most common cognitive distortions (such as overgeneralizing, discounting positives, and emotional reasoning)." They continue, " Each time you notice yourself falling prey to one of them, you name it, describe the facts of the situation, consider alternative interpretations, and then choose an interpretation of events more in line with those facts. Your emotions follow your new interpretation. In time, this process becomes automatic. When people improve their mental hygiene in this way—when they free themselves from the repetitive irrational thoughts that had

Negativity Biases

previously filled so much of their consciousness—they become less depressed, anxious, and angry." In addition, "cognitive behavioral therapy teaches good critical-thinking skills, the sort that educators have striven for so long to impart. By almost any definition, critical thinking requires grounding one's beliefs in evidence rather than in emotion or desire, and learning how to search for and evaluate evidence that might contradict one's initial hypothesis."

I agree with Professors Lukianoff and Haidt's approach, but I believe that you can be your own therapist by doing metacognitive and other exercises. That is why I have written this book.

Exercises III-1A

1. Carefully read each of the items on the Lukianoff and Haidt list. How are they similar to or different from the biases listed in Chapter Two? Which ones do you suffer from; make a list. Be honest! We have all suffered from these negativity biases at one time or another.
2. Write down a list of ways you can overcome your negativity biases. Practice these everyday.
   These specific questions should help you with your list.
3. Think of a situation where you have assumed what someone else was thinking. Did you turn out to be right or wrong? Did your "mind reading" make the situation more difficult?
4. Think of a situation where you practiced fortune-telling? Did things come out as bad as you thought they were going to? If so, <u>is it possible that your negative prophecy was self-fulfilling?</u>
5. Think of a situation in which you catastrophized? Did things turn out as bad as you thought they were going to? Did your catastrophizing make it harder to do the task? Do you generally have problems completing tasks because of catastrophizing?
6. Do you often label yourself? Does labeling yourself cause you problems, such as making it difficult to complete tasks? Do you label others? Do these labels affect how you interact with others? Are these labels generally correct or inaccurate? Do labels negatively affect how you interact with others? Are labels a substitute for treating people as individuals? Are labels a substitute for deep thinking?
7. Do you discount the positive things you do? How does discounting affect your motivation?
8. Do you focus on the negatives? How does this affect your ability to complete projects? How does this affect the quality of your work?
9. Do you overgeneralize? Do you see patterns in specific occurrences? What is the logical error in generalized thinking? How has overgeneralization caused you problems in your professional life?
10. Do you view events or people in all-or-nothing terms? What is the logical error in this type of thinking? Think of several instances in your life where you have used dichotomous thinking. Were you right? What types of problems did dichotomous thinking cause you?
11. Do you blame others for your faults or negative feelings? How does this bias affect your ability to change? How does this affect your ability to complete tasks or the quality of your work?
12. Do you ever use what if thinking? Has this type of thinking caused you not to act when you should have?
13. Do you let your feelings guide your view of reality? Or, do you try to think about your

problems rationally? Write down the ways that emotional thinking can cause problems? Brainstorm!

14. Do you reject any evidence or arguments that might contradict your negative thoughts? Does this bias cause you problems in completing tasks.

15. Do you have a process for making decisions? Having an established decision-making or problem-solving process can help you overcome some of your negativity biases.

16. Problem: Consider whether protestors in the following protests should be arrested. A peaceful protest of President Trump's immigration policies. A peaceful protest outside an abortion clinic. A peaceful protest of President Trump's immigration policies that violates a local law. (Such as protestors must stay on the sidewalks and not enter a street) A peaceful protest outside an abortion clinic that violates a local law. A violent protest of President Trump's immigration policies. A violent protest outside an abortion clinic. Consider how cognitive biases may have affected your answers.

Answer

16. If you were using objective reasoning, your answers should have been the same for both the Trump protest and the abortion center protest. If your answers were different, you suffered from emotional reasoning. Most people are affected by emotional reasoning concerning issues they feel strongly about. Write down times emotional reasoning has affected your reasoning.

Exercises III-1B: Overcoming Negativity Biases

Label the following biases according to the Lukianoff and Haidt list.

1. My wife is a bad driver. All women are bad drivers.
2. I am a poor writer.
3. If I go to the doctor, she will find cancer.
4. Even though I got an A on the first paper, I will probably fail this class.
5. If I ask Debbie for a date, I might get nervous.
6. My boss thinks I am stupid.
7. I failed the exam because the professor is a poor teacher.
8. My boss complimented my work, but that doesn't mean she won't fire me.
9. My children only complain.
10. He's lazy.
11. There's no reason to apply for that job. I won't get it.
12. She is going to complain about me to my boss.
13. I don't like him because he got promoted over me.
14. If I don't get this job, I will never work again.
15. Going to college was a complete waste of time.

Answers

1. Overgeneralizing.

Negativity Biases

2. Labeling.
3. Catastrophizing.
4. Inability to disconfirm.
5. What if.
6. Mind reading.
7. Blaming.
8. Discounting.
9. Negative filtering.
10. Labeling. It's easy to label someone as lazy. Looking at the problem in depth is hard. However, looking at a problem in depth and avoiding labels makes you a better thinker. If you just use labels, you aren't thinking at all.
11. Fortune-telling.
12. Mind reading.
13. Emotional reasoning.
14. Overgeneralizing.
15. Dichotomous thinking.

Now, go back through this exercise and consider the consequences of the negative thinking.

You can overcome some of these negativity biases by creating a positive mental picture to counter the negativity. For example, instead of catastrophizing or fortune-telling, picture what success might look like. For instance, think of a high school dance, a social situation which causes many teens great anxiety. Instead of picturing everything that can go wrong, picture yourself having a good time. Think of yourself dancing with your boyfriend. Think of yourself and others laughing. Similarly, instead of labeling yourself with negative traits, think of the positive characteristics you have, then think about what these traits mean and how others perceive them.

B. Negativity Biases in Legal Practice

Negativity biases can be just as damaging for lawyers as the optimism biases we discussed in the previous chapter. To begin with, write down all the negativity biases that have affected you as a lawyer and how they affected you.

Examples.
I lost the case because my associate didn't do enough research. (blaming)
All associates are lazy. (dichotomous thinking or overgeneralizing)
I am depressed because I am a poor lawyer. (emotional reasoning)
My boss thinks I am a poor lawyer. (mind reading)
There is no reason to file suit; we can't win the case (fortune-telling) (Notice that this is the opposite of an optimism bias.)
If I lose the case, my firm will fire me. (catastrophizing)
No one in the firm thinks I'm a good lawyer. (negative filtering)
If I lose this case, I probably will be fired. Then, I will lose my home, and my wife will leave me. (what if?)

Can you see how the above negativity biases might affect your ability to function as a lawyer? How they might lead to other problems, such as drug use, alcoholism, or depression? You should take a realistic view of things, but never focus on the negative. If you are focusing on the negatives, write out a list that contains both the positives and negatives of a situation. If you lose a case, think about all the cases you have won. All people have problems in their lives, but they also have good things, too.

II. Mindfulness/Well-Being and Overcoming the Negativity Bias

As you can see from the above, negativity is very damaging for lawyers. Many researchers have suggested that mindfulness can lessen negativity biases.[14] Cognitive science studies have demonstrated that stress and related emotions can diminish cognitive performance.[15] In fact, one scientist called anxiety "a transient learning disability that interferes with a student's working memory and ability to complete tasks."[16] Consequently, people need techniques for diminishing stress and the other negative emotions in their lives.

According to two authors, "Mindfulness [a restorative practice] is a sustained, receptive attention to and awareness of events and experiences as they occur. That is, it involves a regulation of attention and awareness toward present-moment experiences. Furthermore, these observations are made in a nondiscriminatory fashion, that is, they are experienced simply as they occur rather than selectively avoiding some and dwelling in others. Such receptivity is necessary to truly orient attention toward whatever the present moment holds. This process entails a reduction in habitual mental elaboration on thoughts and feelings about experiences, freeing conscious resources to process information that is immediate to the present moment."[17] "A rich theoretical literature suggests that the receptive nature of mindfulness reframes observations so that they are clearer and less biased."[18] This may be due to the fact that mindfulness "free[s] resources, allowing for greater attention to and awareness of positive information."[19]

The key to developing mindfulness is to draw on intrinsic values, rather than external stimuli or motivation. As Professor Larry Krieger has declared, "The former values direct one towards self-understanding, close relationships with others, prosocial/helping outcomes, and community improvement, while the latter embody a more contingent worth, external rewards orientation–toward money, luxuries, influence and appearance." For example, "one is intrinsically motivated when he chooses an action which he genuinely enjoys or which furthers a fundamental life purpose, while extrinsically motivated choices are directed towards external rewards (i.e. money, grades, honors), avoidance of guilt or fear, or pleasing/impressing others."[20] He added, "Empirical research for the past two decades has consistently shown that intrinsic values and motivation, when primary in a person's value system, produce satisfaction and well-being, whereas when extrinsic values and motivation are primary they produce angst and distress."[21]

Similarly, Professor Martin Seligman describes the basis of well-being, "Authentic happiness comes from identifying your most fundamental strengths and using them every day in work, love, play, and parenting."[22] Finally, two professors have written, "Human beings also have a deep-rooted and fundamental desire for meaning in terms of making sense of their lives."[23]

Negativity Biases

Exercise III-2A

Write down what you think your eulogy will be when given by a relative or a friend.[24]

Comments on Exercise

The purpose of this exercise is to determine what you value in your life. Professor Krieger noted, "It turns out that the qualities and values typically expressed in these eulogies are the most traditional human values and virtues: patience, decency, humility, courage, caring, integrity, willingness to work hard for worthwhile goals, helpfulness to others (family, friends, clients or community), and so forth. No one thus far in my experience has drafted a eulogy about a luxurious home, high grade point average or exceptionally lucrative law practice."[25]

Professor Krieger concluded, "If you focus your life on gaining wealth, popularity, prestige, or influence, you are making a mistake (assuming you want to feel satisfied with your life). If you focus your life on growth, integrity, compassion and respectfulness on the levels of your self (which includes honoring your values and heeding your conscience), your personal and professional relationships, and your community interactions–your life will feel meaningful and satisfying. You will avoid the frustration, isolation, emptiness, compulsions and addictions common to many in our society and our profession. And as a side benefit, you will also undoubtedly grow in comforts beyond your needs, because your right choices will create positive outcomes and good will."[26]

Exercise III-2B: Your Well-Being

Consider the following questions. There are no correct answers.

1. Professors Ryff and Keyes write that well-being consists of 1) self-acceptance, 2) environmental mastery, 3) purpose in life, 4) positive relations with others, 5) personal growth, and 6) autonomy.[27] Rate yourself on each of these factors.
2. What gives you satisfaction? What gives your life meaning?
3. Do you enjoy your job? What do you enjoy the most about your job? The least? Why did you choose your profession? Do you get meaning from being a lawyer, or is it just a way to earn a living? If you said just earning a living, come up with a plan to get more satisfaction from being a lawyer.
4. Are you satisfied with your personal life? How has being a lawyer affected your personal life?
5. Do you have lots of friends? How do you feel about this?
6. Why did you choose your major in college? Did you enjoy college? Why did you choose your courses in college–because they were interesting, because they would help you in your career, or because they were easy?
7. Why did you choose the type of law you are practicing?
8. Are your motivations in school or your job intrinsic, or extrinsic, or both? (be specific)
9. How can you better develop your intrinsic motivators?
10. Do you like working with people? How does this relate to being a lawyer?

10. Do you like helping others? How does this relate to being a lawyer?
11. Do you like intellectual things? How does this relate to being a lawyer?
12. Is your well-being important to others?

Getting more satisfaction from being a lawyer.
1. Write down the good you accomplished as a lawyer. Find one good thing you have done everyday. ("I helped my client to plan for his future with an estate plan." "I kept an innocent man out of jail." "Even though my client was guilty, I limited the amount of time she will spend in jail." "I helped a business that is important to the community survive.")
2. Act ethically. Unethical behavior causes negative feelings.
3. Be positive without being unrealistic.
4. Develop a growth mindset. (see below)
5. Make sure you take some time off every week.
6. Make sure you spend time with friends and family every week.
7. Do pro bono. Helping others feels good; it causes the brain to make dopamine.
8. If things get overwhelming seek help! There is no shame in seeking help.

'Work-life balance obviously has a strong effect on a lawyer's or law student's well-being. Professors Krieger and Sheldon have found these work-life factors to be important:[28]

1. Physical exercise contributes to well-being.
2. Taking vacations is important for well-being.
3. Excessive alcohol use inhibits well-being.
4. Hours worked had no appreciable effect on well-being.
5. Keeping track of hours worked (in those professions that track such things) causes a slight decrease in happiness.
6. Charity work contributes to well-being.
7. Married persons have greater well-being.

Exercise III-2C: Well-Being

1. Make a list of things that negatively affect your well-being?
2. Do you exercise?
3. Are vacations important to you?
4. Do you think you have achieved balance between your job and your personal life?
5. Are you depressed? Do you have trouble sleeping? Do you drink too much?
6. Do you take time to have fun?
7. Do you take time to be with friends?
8. Do you talk about your problems with your friends?
9. Is there any thing wrong with seeing a counselor if you need one?
10. Have you ever considered joining a self-help group?

Recommended Reading

Negativity Biases

Jonathan Haidt, The Happiness Hypothesis: Finding Modern Truth in Ancient Wisdom (2006).

III. The Growth Mindset and The Fixed Mindset

The fixed mindset is probably the most pernicious of all the negativity biases. It affects both law students and lawyers. A fixed mindset is the belief that intelligence is fixed and cannot be improved. Having this negative cognitive bias can interfere with your ability to learn and succeed in life. The way to overcome it is by developing a "growth mindset."

The growth mindset is "based on the belief that your basic qualities are things you can cultivate through your efforts."[29] People who have growth mindsets succeed at learning and the other parts of life.

Questions III-3A: The Growth Mindset

1. Do you have a growth mindset or a fixed one? In other words, do you think you can improve your intelligence and ability to learn?
2. Do you tackle or avoid difficult problems?
3. Has anyone labeled you as a poor learner?
4. Are you a lazy learner?
5. Are you afraid of making mistakes?
6. Do you like to try new things?

A major impediment preventing many people from succeeding is that they have the mindset that intelligence is fixed–that humans are born with a level of intelligence that is unchangeable during their lifetimes. If intelligence is unchangeable, why should I work hard? Recent research has shown that the fixed mindset is not correct, but that with hard work and the proper approach a normal person can increase their intelligence (fluid or malleable intelligence).[30] As a leading expert in this field has stated, "[t]he view you adopt for yourself profoundly affects the way you lead your life."[31]

Scientific research supports the growth mindset. The question of whether intelligence is nature (genetics) or nurture (environment) is easily answerable: it is both.[32] Scientists used to think that intelligence was 50% genetics and 50% environment.[33] Today, many believe that intelligence is probably more environment than genetics.[34] Regardless of who is right, intelligence is at least 50% environment (learning). Consequently, "*[i]ntelligence is malleable. It can be improved.*"[35] You can succeed if you believe you can succeed.[36]

For example, working memory use can be improved through attention and motivation. Similarly, long-term memory, which is vital to thinking and learning, can be vastly improved through repetition and retrieval.

Students who believe that intelligence is malleable get higher grades than those who don't,[37] so you must convince yourself that the right kind of hard work pays off. As one scholar has declared, "[m]indsets are beliefs. They're powerful beliefs, but they're just something in your mind, and you can change your mind."[38] The major way of accepting that intelligence is fluid is to address your beliefs directly.[39] First, "[j]ust by knowing about the two mindsets you can think about reacting in a new way."[40] Another way to help yourself understand that intelligence is malleable is to think of examples of famous scientists, athletes, authors, and entertainers who have succeed through hard work.[41] Moreover, you need to convince yourself that failure is part of learning–that even the greatest scientists failed before they achieved success.[42] As one scholar has noted, "[t]hose with the growth mindset kept on learning. Not worried about measuring–or protecting–their fixed abilities, they looked directly at their mistakes, used the feedback, and altered their strategies accordingly."[43]

However, you still need to have a realistic picture of your abilities, or you will tackle tasks that are too hard. Harder tasks can be saved for when you have mastered simpler ones. Similarly, a belief that intelligence is fixed can also have a negative affect on students who are labeled as intelligent. When such a student receives a poor grade, she will often attribute it to inaccurate grading or prejudice from the teacher, rather than the fact that she didn't work hard enough or that she took the wrong approach.[44] Thus, she will not change her approach or work harder.[45]

Exercises III-3B: The Growth Mindset

1. Think about instances in your past when you have gotten better at something. What caused this improvement?
2. Consider your past successes. Were you just lucky, or did you succeed through hard work?

Notes

1. *Negativity Bias*, Good Theraphy Org. [http://www.goodtherapy.org/blog/psychpedia/negativity-bias].

2. Amrisha Vaish et.al., *Not all emotions are created equal: The negativity bias in social-emotional development*, 134 Psychol Bull. 383 (may 2008). [https://www.ncbi.nlm.nih.gov/pmc/articles/PMC3652533/]; Daniel Kahneman, Thinking, Fast and Slow 300 (2011) ([N]egativity and escape dominate positivity and approach.").

3. *Id.* at 301.

4. Greg Lukianoff and Jonathan Haidt, *The Coddling of the American Mind*,
The Atlantic (Sept 15 2015). [http://www.theatlantic.com/magazine/archive/2015/09/] Based on Robert L. Leahy, Stephen J. F. Holland, and Lata K. McGinn's Treatment Plans and Interventions for Depression and Anxiety Disorders (2012).

5. Lukianoff & Haidt, *supra*.

6. Rick Hanson, *Confronting the Negativity Bias*, [http://www.rickhanson.net/how-your-brain-makes-you-easily-intimidated/; *see also* Kahneman, *supra* at 301.

7. Rick Hanson, *supra*.

8. *Id.*

9. *Id.*

10. Kahneman, *supra* at 301.

11. Lukianoff & Haidt, *supra*.

12. *Id.*

13. *Id.*

14. Laura G. Kiken & Natalie J. Shook, *Looking Up: Mindfulness Increases Positive Judgments and Reduces Negativity Bias*, 2 Social Psychological and Personality Science 425 (2011). [https://www.researchgate.net/profile/Natalie_Shook/publication/258189450_Looking_Up/links/0deec539b49f00001d000000.pdf]

15. Debra S. Austin, *Positive Legal Education: Flourishing Law Students and Thriving Law Schools*, 5,8. [https://papers.ssrn.com/sol3/papers.cfm?abstract_id=2928329]

16. *Id.* at 16.

17. Kiken & Shook, *supra*.

18. *Id.*

19. *Id.*

20. Lawrence S. Krieger, *The Inseparability of Professionalism and Personal Satisfaction*. [http://papers.ssrn.com/sol3/papers.cfm?abstract_id=549361&download=yes at 1 (2004).

21. *Id.*

22. Martin E.P. Seligman, Authentic Happiness: Using the New Positive Psychology to Realize Your Potential for Lasting Fulfillment xiii (2002).

23. Peter H. Huang & Rick Swedloff, Authentic Happiness and Meaning at Law Firms, http://www.researchgate.net/profile/Peter_Huang5/publication/228222844_Authentic_Happiness_and_Meaning_at_Law_Firms/links/02e7e521ae84a92256000000.pdf at 5 (2008).

24. Krieger, *supra*.

25. *Id.*

26. *Id.* at 3.

27. Carol D. Ryff & Corey Lee M. Keyes, The Structure of Psychological Well-Being Revisited, 69 J. Personality & Soc. Psych. 720 (1995).

28. Lawrence S. Krieger & Kennon M. Sheldon, What Makes Lawyers Happy?: A Data-Driven Prescription to Redefine Professional Success, http://papers.ssrn.com/sol3/papers.cfm?abstract_id=239898 (2015).

29. Carol S. Dweck, Mindset: The New Psychology of Success 7 (2006). Dweck added, "[d]o people with this mindset believe that anyone can be anything, that anyone with the proper motivation or education can become Einstein or Beethoven? No, but they believe that a person's true potential is unknown (and unknowable); that it's impossible to foresee what can be accomplished with years of passion, toil, and training." *Id.*

30. Susan A. Ambrose et.al., How Learning Works: 7 Research-Based Principles for Smart Teaching 200-201 (2010); Daniel T. Willingham, Why Don't Students Like School? 169-87 (2009); *see generally* Geoff Colvin, Talent is Overrated: What Really Separates World-Class Performers from Everybody Else 23 (2008).Colvin, *supra* note 23 ("The research finds that in many fields the relation between intelligence and performance is weak or nonexistent; people with modest IQs sometimes perform outstandingly while people with high IQs sometimes don't get past mediocrity." *Id.* at 51.).

31. Dweck, *supra*.

32. Willingham, *supra* at 169; Dweck, *supra* at 5.

33. Willingham, *supra* note 6, at 175-76.

34. *Id.* at 177-79.

35. *Id.* at 179.

36. Of course, you must also work hard and improve yourself using the right methods.

37. Willingham, *supra* at 180. Professor Dweck relates that a mindset workshop had a significant impact on students' learning and grades. Dweck, *supra* at 215 ("This one adjustment of students' beliefs seemed to unleash the brain power and inspire them to work and achieve.").

38. Dweck, *supra* at 16.

39. Ambrose, *supra* at 212.

40. Dweck, *supra* at 46; *see also id.* at 212-15.

41. Willingham, *supra* note 6, at 183.

42. *Id.* at 184.

43. Dweck, *supra* at 111.

44. Ambrose, *supra* at 201.

45. *Id.*

Chapter Four
Biases Concerning Others

Chapter Goals.
1. To discuss biases concerning others in detail.
2. To give the reader ways to deal with biases against others.

     Lawyers frequently deal with other people–attorneys, judges, clients, support staff, etc. However, many studies have shown that cognitive biases can affect how we perceive people, and, therefore, how we deal with them. A good attorney tries to overcome her cognitive biases when dealing with others.

     Here are biases that concern how humans perceive or deal with others:

1. Bandwagon effect: "The tendency to do (or believe) things because many other people do (or believe) the same."
2. Bias blind spot: "The tendency to see oneself as less biased than other people, or to be able to identify more cognitive biases in others than in oneself."
3. Empathy gap: "The tendency to underestimate the influence or strength of feelings, in either oneself or others."
4. Essentialism: "Categorizing people and things according to their essential nature, in spite of variations."
5. Halo effect: "The tendency for a person's positive or negative traits to 'spill over' from one personality area to another in others' perceptions of them."
6. Identifiable-victim effect: "The tendency to respond more strongly to a single identified person at risk than to a large group of people at risk."
7. In-group bias: "The tendency for people to give preferential treatment to others they perceive to be members of their own groups."
8. Projection bias: "The tendency to unconsciously assume that others (or one's future selves) share one's current emotional states, thoughts and values."[1]

I. Halo Effect

     Halo effect: "The tendency for a person's positive or negative traits to 'spill over' from one personality area to another in others' perceptions of them."[2] It is "the tendency to use global evaluations to make judgments about specific traits."[3] It is an excellent example of a heuristic, which I discussed in Chapter One. The effect can also apply to other things, such as companies, products, brands, or entities.
     A frequent example of the halo effect is attributing positive traits to persons because of their attractiveness.[4] Thus, humans attribute personality traits to individuals they have seen, but never met.[5]

Examples.
I wish I were friends with my favorite actress. She is so attractive, and I bet she is really friendly.

Understanding and Overcoming Cognitive Biases for Lawyers and Law Students

Teacher: The new boy is the handsomest student I have ever seen. He must be really smart.
Studies have shown that attractive teachers get better evaluations than average-looking ones.
I'll vote for that candidate because he is the most attractive.
Let's hire that candidate as our new CEO. He has the best hair. (A Dilbert joke.)
I'll choose this breakfast cereal. It has the coolest box.
I like the way that car looks. It must be reliable.
I'll buy that car because I like their racing team.
She is very intelligent. She must have a great personality.
He is intelligent. He must be a good leader.
She is really intelligent. I can't wait to hear her piano recital.
Negative halo effect: That man looks grumpy.

From the above, it is obvious that the halo effect can be a harmful bias. It causes humans to judge others based on a single trait. Thus, an unattractive teacher may receive a low evaluation from students just because she is unattractive.

Possible causes.
1. Heuristic thinking. "When information is scarce, . . . System 1 operates as a machine for jumping to conclusions."[6]
2. Emotional thinking.
3. The tendency to judge based on first impressions. System 1 gives greater weight to traits observed first.[7]

Lawyers need to see their clients objectively; they cannot let the halo effect color how they deal with a client. For example, lawyers must be able to determine when their client isn't telling the truth. If the truth comes out later, it may damage a case or a negotiation.

Legal Examples.
My client does a lot of charity work. I'm sure he gave me all the relevant documents.
My client is a famous athlete, he must be telling the truth.
This associate did well in law school. I can trust him with the Lawson brief, even though he is inexperienced.
Hiring an assistant because he is handsome.

Overcoming the Halo Effect

1. Awareness of the halo effect.
2. Slow down and use System 2.
3. Get more information before making a judgment about a person.
4. Get more information before making a judgment about a product or a company.
5. Consider carefully what your opinion of a person is based on.
6. Avoid global judgments based on limited evidence.

Kahneman uses "decorrelatiing error" to overcome the halo effect.[8] When multiple sources exist, keep the sources independent of each other. For example, to avoid early speakers from overinfluencing a meeting, have each of the participants write down a summary of their opinions before the meeting.

Exercises IV-1

1. Have you ever judged a person by the halo effect? How did this affect your view of this individual? Looking back, was your assessment accurate?
2. Have you seen the halo effect in others? How did it affect their judgment?
3. Do you think you have ever been treated unfairly because of the halo effect?
4. Think of instances where you initially judged a person negatively, but later formed a positive view of that person. Now, do the opposite.
5. Have you noticed how news outlets often use unattractive pictures of people they are criticizing? Why do they do this?
6. Has the halo effect ever influenced how you handled a case? How can you overcome the halo effect in your practice?

II. Bandwagon Effect

Bandwagon effect: "The tendency to do (or believe) things because many other people do (or believe) the same."[9] (Peer pressure) According to researchers, "attitudes and behavior are influenced by how we view other people."[10] The bandwagon effect can occur quickly, but it can disappear as quickly as trends change.[11]

Examples.
Voting for a candidate because all your friends are planning to vote for her.
Voting for a candidate because he is leading in the polls.
Dressing a certain way because your friends dress the same way.
Liking a song because your friends like the song.
It must be the best restaurant in town; everyone is going there.
I should buy that stock; all my friends are.
I've decided to start smoking because all the cool kids are doing it.

Of course, maybe everyone is going to that restaurant because it is the best one in town. The key is to look at your judgments critically to determine whether they are based on a bias or your best judgment (System 2).

Legal Examples.
Agreeing with the other attorneys concerning the strategy of a case. "Yes men" lead to poor results because the best decision is made after weighing the alternatives.
Going to law school because all of your friends are going to law school.
Voting a lawyer partnership, even though you have serious doubts about him.

Possible causes.

Understanding and Overcoming Cognitive Biases for Lawyers and Law Students

1. People prefer to conform. It is less stressful.
2. People derive information from others.
3. Social pressure.[12]

Overcoming the Bandwagon Effect

1. Ask whether you are making the decision based on your judgment or the opinion of others.
2. Make sure you have all relevant information.
3. Ask whether you are bowing to peer pressure.

Exercises IV-2

1. List instances when you have suffered from the bandwagon effect? Were you using System 1 or 2? Would your judgment have been different if you had thought about the situation more?
2. List several fads you have observed. (When I was young the hula hoop was a big fad. It lasted a few months, then everyone stopped buying hula hoops.)
3. In the fall of 2016, many people became Cubs fans. Why do you think this happened?
4. List the possible harmful effects of the bandwagon effect.
5. Has the bandwagon effect affected you in practice? How?
6. How can a law firm discourage yes men and encourage open dialogue?

III. Empathy Gap

Lawyers need to understand their client's emotions and the emotions of others. Is my client acting rationally, or is he acting based on his emotions? Is the opposing attorney acting rationally, or is he acting based on his emotions?

Empathy gap: "The tendency to underestimate the influence or strength of feelings, in either oneself or others."[13] Similarly, "Where people in one state of mind fail to understand people in another state of mind."[14]

An essential part of dealing with others is the ability to estimate others' psychological states and how others respond to those states.[15] "However, when others are in different situations from oneself—and especially when those situations evoke different emotional states—the assumption that others' attitudes, preferences, and behaviors are the same as one's own can lead to biased, ill-considered, and regrettable social behavior."[16] The empathy gap occurs because 1) "people often assume and overestimate the similarity between themselves and others" and 2) "any bias in prediction of their own reactions to different emotional situations would cause them to make correspondingly biased estimates of other people's reactions to those situations."[17]

Researchers have found two types of empathy gaps. "Cold–hot empathy gaps occur when people in relatively neutral 'cold' situations predict their reactions to emotional 'hot' situations. . . . Hot–cold empathy gaps occur when people in emotionally aroused hot states predict their attitudes, preferences, and behaviors in unemotional cold states."[18]

Examples of cold-hot.

Biases Concerning Others

A doctor has trouble evaluating the pain a patient is experiencing. (Cold-hot)
A person who is not in love has a problems considering how a person in love feels. (Cold-hot)
A professor being unsympathetic to the request of a student for an extension on a paper when that student has recently lost a parent. (Cold-hot)
Buying too many groceries when hungry. (Hot-cold)
A drug addict is unable to understand a person who is not addicted to drugs. (Hot-cold)

Examples of empathy gap.
Teachers reacting with harsh criticism to students who are anxious about public speaking.
"The employer who fails to appreciate the added stress on employees of an increased workload may fail to anticipate, and hence, take efforts to allay, employee dissatisfaction."
"The policy maker who fails to appreciate the impact of addiction and craving on drug addicts' behavior may implement policies that exaggerate the addicts' ability to take control of their habit."[19]
A mother deals with her daughter's social problems in high school from the perspective of how things were when she was in high school.
Problems with integrating people from different cultures into new countries.

Examples of empathy-gap in law practice.
Why does she keep crying? We can get two million dollars in a settlement for her husband's wrongful death.
Failing to recognize that a client wants to get revenge on an opponent.
Failing to recognize the emotional traumas of a divorce.
While having an argument in front of a judge, failing to recognize that the judge is becoming angry.

After reading the above examples, can you see how this cognitive bias might affect you as an attorney?

To deal successfully with others, one must develop "emotional perspective taking."[20] This "requires people to recognize that other people are often in emotional situations that are different from their own current situations, to make reasonable estimates about the emotional states evoked by those situations, and to predict how those emotional states will influence other people's attitudes, preferences, and behaviors. That is, successful emotional perspective taking requires predictions both of how different situations evoke emotions in other people and of how other people respond to those emotions."[21] Emotional perspective taking involves two judgments: 1) "people estimate how they themselves would react to an emotional situation different from the one they are currently in" and 2) "they adjust these self-estimates to accommodate perceived differences or similarities between themselves and others."[22]

The projection bias is part of the empathy gap so I will give examples of it here.

Examples of projection.
"[B]ecause people generally believe that they see the world objectively and accurately, they

assume that other people will hold similar perceptions, so long as others are as reasonable and unbiased as the self."[23]

Students who cheat believe a high percentage of students cheat.
People who smoke believe more people smoke than actually do.
I favor that candidate so other rational people do, too.
A bully fails to see the effect on his victim.
I will still like spicy food when I am 80.
If I were my client, I would accept the offer.
The judge will agree with my argument. (This one is especially dangerous because it can lead to the overconfidence effect.)

When I was in graduate school a friend often accused others of projecting their feelings, biases, etc. on others. He had a projection bias about projection.

Overcoming the Empathy Gap

1. Adopt emotional perspective taking.
2. Try to put yourself in the shoes of the other person. (mentally trade places)
3. Try to "visualize" what the other person is going through. Try to predict how others might feel.
4. Don't assume that everyone experiences the same emotions to a particular stimuli.
5. Consider other peoples' emotions when evaluating their behavior. Consider how your decisions affect others.
6. Try to separate your emotions from your decision-making.

Advantages of Overcoming the Empathy Gap[24]

1. A salesman can make more sales if she understands the customers. (Ex. A man buying a diamond ring for his wife.)
2. Negotiators can reach better settlements.
3. Fewer relationship problems.
4. Better teacher evaluations.
5. Regulators make better public policy evaluations.
6. A lawyer will have happier clients and more repeat business.
7. A lawyer will win more cases because she will understand how emotions affect others.

Studies have shown that individuals of one sex have a harder time mentally trading places with members of the other sex, than they do with their own.[25] In other words, it takes more effort to mentally trade places with someone who is very different from you, but it can be done to a certain extent.

The empathy gap can also affect an individual's well-being. For example, many people underestimate the social embarrassment of themselves compared to other people, concluding that they have less social courage than others.[26] Moreover, people have trouble predicting how they will feel in different emotional states.[27] For instance, in the hot-cold state, people "believe they are acting more dispassionately than they actually are," which can lead to crimes of passion.[28]

Exercises IV-3

1. How often do you allow emotions to affect your thinking? Do you assume that others share the same preferences as you?
2. Think how the empathy gap has caused you problems. How could you have handled those situations better?
3. Imagine that you are a parent and that your child has just broken a valuable vase. Considering the empathy gap, how should you deal with your child?
4. Imagine you have just been in a traffic accident, which you think was the other driver's fault. What is the best way to deal with this situation?
5. You are the boss on an important project that is due at the end of the day. A key employee comes to you and asks to leave work because her son has just been in a traffic accident. What would you do? (Reimagine this scenario from multiple viewpoints. What if the accident is minor. What if the boy's father is already taking care of things? What if, instead of an accident, the son has a cold?)
6. You have a new employee who keeps messing up? How do you deal with the problem?
7. Take a common problem like same-sex marriage, affirmative action, pregnancy benefits. Think how you feel about that problem. Then, think about the problem from the prospect of an individual of a different race, sex, or sexual orientation.
8. Have you ever overreacted, such as getting into a fight, because of the empathy gap? How could you have handled the situation differently?
9. One of your employees, Jessica, is being difficult today. Think of all the possible bases for her behavior. Brainstorm, then be critical of your answers.
10. Your spouse is in a bad mood. You wonder what you have done. Think of all the possible bases for her behavior. Brainstorm, then be critical of your answers. Can you now see that maybe it isn't your fault?
11. Think of an instance when someone didn't answer an important email for several days. Why did that person fail to answer the email? Were they mad at you? Irresponsible? Something else?
12. Has the empathy gap affected your practice? How?
13. Have you ever suffered from an empathy gap or projection bias when dealing with a client? How did it affect your relationship with the client?
14. Have you ever suffered from an empathy gap or projection bias when dealing with a judge? How did it affect your case?

IV. Bias Blind Spot

Bias blind spot: "The tendency to see oneself as less biased than other people, or to be able to identify more cognitive biases in others than in oneself."[29] Most of us believe that we are less biased than other people. Is this true? No, researchers have established that everyone has a bias blind spot to some degree.[30] People have difficulty acting objectively. This applies even to cognitively-sophisticated people.[31]

Examples.
People who point out racial biases in others, but who can't see them in themselves.
Blaming the coach for playing his son too much, but doing the same thing when you take over the team.
Doctors accepting gifts from drug companies, believing that the gift won't influence their drug choices but might influence other doctors' choices.
Politicians who take campaign donations, believing that they can avoid being influenced by the donation.
A male cop who doesn't realize why he didn't give an attractive woman a ticket.
A lawyer who handles a case differently because the client is of a different race.

Probable causes.
1. People view themselves positively, and biases are considered undesirable.
2. People are unaware of unconscious processes (System 1) and therefore cannot see their influence in the decision-making process.
3. People are often unable to control their blind spot biases even when they are informed they have them.[32]

A pair of authors have conjectured that blind spot biases are due to the "introspection illusion."[33] They believe that individuals use overt behavior when determining whether a person is biased, but they use introspection when evaluating themselves. This introspection is unhelpful because biases are unconscious.

Overcoming the Bias Blind Spot

1. Become more self-aware. Reflect on your actions.
2. Be totally honest with yourself. Realize that you are human and that you make mistakes and have shortcomings.
3. Use System 2 when evaluating yourself. Don't be a cognitive miser. (Don't go for the first solution.)

Exercises IV-4

1. Think of times you have suffered from the bias blind spot? How wrong were you? What effect did the bias have?
2. Do you think you can observe biases in others? What is your thinking process in evaluating biases in others? How does it differ from your thinking process in evaluating your biases?
3. Quickly write down ten things you think about members of another racial group. Now evaluate your list critically for unconscious biases. Do the same thing with members of the opposite sex, members of a different sexual orientation, religion. Next, do the same exercise for an individual you know in one of those groups.
4. Think of a sports team you hate. Quickly write down characteristics of fans of that team.

Biases Concerning Others

Now, critically evaluate the list for biases.
5. Think of the way that bias blind spots can affect you in practice/
6. Do you treat lawyers of the opposite sex the same way you do lawyers of your sex?
7. Do you treat lawyers of a different racial group the same way as lawyers of your racial group?
8. How would you feel if a transgendered person applied for a job with your law firm?

V. Identifiable-Victim Effect

Identifiable-victim effect: "The tendency to respond more strongly to a single identified person at risk than to a large group of people at risk." Studies have shown that "a neurobehavioral mechanism underlying the identifiable victim effect by demonstrating that affect [emotion] elicited by identifiable information reliably shifts preferences for giving."[34] This effect is caused by affect (emotions). A single victim bridges the emotion gap, it increases the feeling of impact, and it connects supporters to a story in motion.[35] In other words, "a story is more emotionally engaging than a set of statistics."[36] Statistics don't generate emotions, and unconscious emotions can be stronger than logic.

Examples.
Making all efforts to save a child who is missing, while not expending resources to protect children from abduction in general.
A charity uses a poster child to help it collect money.
Sending money to a fund to help a victim of spousal abuse you saw on tv, rather than an established charity to help battered women.

This bias might actually be good for a lawyer. It might cause him to fight harder for the client. However, an attorney must be careful to not let this cause her to overstep ethical bounds.

Overcoming the Identifiable-Victim Effect

1. Being aware of the effect.
2. Ask whether logic or emotion is driving your decision-making process.
3. Using analytical processing (System 2).

Exercises IV-5

1. Think of instances where you have suffered from the identifiable victim effect? Are you more likely to donate to an identifiable victim or a charity that helps people in general?
2. Can the identifiable-victim effect be useful in some situations? Have you seen such situations in the news?
3. Which is worse--a child in your community who lost his parents in a traffic accident, or thousands of children in the Middle East who have been orphaned by war?
4. Has this bias ever affected you in practice? How?

VI. Essentialism

The essentialism bias can produce narrow reasoning in a lawyer. Essentialism: "Categorizing people and things according to their essential nature, in spite of variations." Essentialism has several different meanings, but I want to focus on the one in the previous sentence, which is a cognitive bias. As one can see from this definition alone, this bias can be an impediment to clear thinking.

Essentialism is a type of generalization that helps humans learn. It is easier to fit things into clear categories than to learn all the detailed variations among things.[37] Moreover, "essentialism is a 'placeholder' notion: one can believe that a category possesses an essence without knowing what the essence is."[38] In other words, humans often attribute characteristics to a category that they don't actually observe.

However, essentialism can cause someone to ignore the essential qualities of an individual or thing. It can lead to stereotyping. It can also lead to dangerous decision-making. For example, "Genocide is perpetrated by individuals who dehumanize or define the victims as essentially different and/or contaminated."[39]

Examples.
Jennifer can't be a soldier. She is a woman, and woman are too weak to fight in wars.
He is from a poor neighborhood so he should set his career sights low.
All Martians vote Republican.
He is a Martian so he must be good at math.
An individual is stuck with the intelligence she inherited from her parents. She can do nothing about it. (Also growth mindset)
We should treat all alcoholics the same.
Don't represent Martians; they are difficult clients.
Martians are dumb so I will have to dumb things down for this client. (Boy, can this one get you in trouble.)
The judge is a Martian; there is no way I can win this case.
Doctors should treat all cancer patients the same.

Overcoming Essentialism

1. Realizing that categories are generalizations to help us think more easily. (a heuristic) Focus on individual differences.
2. Question inductive thinking. (Aristotle is a man. All men are mortal. Aristotle is mortal. The problem here is a failure to question the premises. Aristotle is a man. All men have thick hair on their heads. Aristotle has thick hair on his head. The problem here is with the minor premise; some men are bald.)
3. Don't assume that a member of a group shares all the characteristics of that group.
4. Don't jump to conclusions. Gather all the information that is needed to make an informed decision.

Exercises IV-6

Biases Concerning Others

1. What are the main biological differences between a Caucasian and an African-American? Only one thing–skin color.
2. Think of all the jobs that women are usually disqualified for? Do you know any woman who could do those jobs?
3. Think of times you have been guilty of essentialism? Have you ever attributed characteristics to a person when you haven't actually seen the characteristics in that person?
4. Do Republicans suffer from essentialism? Do Democrats?
5. How is essentialism like the halo effect?
6. Have you ever "stereotyped" a client? How did this affect your dealings with the client?
7. Have you ever thought that essentialism might influence a jury in one of your cases? What can you do to avoid this?
8. Consider how essentialism can be a problem in employment law.
9. How has essentialism affected divorce, child custody, alimony, and property settlements. Have both men and women gotten "bad deals" in family law disputes because of essentialism?
10. Should courts be reluctant to place a black child with a white family? Should a court be reluctant to place a white child with a black family?

VII. In-Group Bias

Treating those in your group better than outsiders can cause many problems for attorneys. In-group bias: "The tendency for people to give preferential treatment to others they perceive to be members of their own groups." "Social structure and individual psychology converge to make ingroup-outgroup differentiation an inevitable feature of social life."[40] While this bias often involves racial, ethnic, or religious groups, it can involve any type of group. A person can be a member of several in-groups.

The in-group bias can be a positive trait: "preferential positivity toward ingroups does not necessarily imply negativity or hostility toward outgroups."[41] Discrimination to those outside the group can be based on in-group preference, without any hostility toward the out-group.[42] While in-groups vary depending on local conditions or individual needs, "Wherever drawn, however, ingroup-outgroup distinctions shape social interactions and opportunities for cooperation, imitation, and interdependence."[43] In-group members share values.[44]

In-groups are evolutionary; "group living represents the fundamental survival strategy. . ." for humans (obligatory interdependence).[45] Thus, in-groups are "communities of mutual trust and obligation that delimit mutual interdependence and cooperation."

While there is not necessarily hostility of the in-group to the out-group, maintaining group integrity and loyalty may produce moral superiority, distrust, and perceived threat.[46] Of course, this can create serious discrimination from one group's members to another's.

Examples.
Martians versus non-Martians
Nerds versus jocks
Engineers versus scientists
Yankees fans versus Red Sox fans
Democrats versus Republicans

Understanding and Overcoming Cognitive Biases for Lawyers and Law Students

A club's members
A gang
Bowling teams
Fraternities
A college's students
Community-police relationships
Dog people versus cat people
Doctors, lawyers, nurses, fireman, any job
Treating lawyers with more respect than other people.
Rejecting ideas from associates from a different racial group

Possible causes.[47]
1. Competition for scarce resources.
2. Self-interest.
3. Self-esteem–"The desire to view one's self positively is transferred onto the group."
4. Oxytocin–"oxytocin [a brain hormone] enables the development of trust, specifically towards individuals with similar characteristics - categorized as 'in-group' members - promoting cooperation with and favoritism towards such individuals."

Overcoming an In-Group Bias

1. Awareness.
2. Relying on judgement, rather than heuristics. Understanding the out-group in detail. Trying to see things from the perspective of the out-group.
3. Breaking down or eliminating categories. (Ex. A post-racial America)
4. Creating cross-groups. (Bringing together members of different racial groups as members of a sports team or a club. Ex. Conductor, Daniel Barenboim and Professor Edward Said founded the West-Eastern Divan Orchestra in 1999 to bring together Israeli, Palestinian, and other Arab musicians. "Within the workshop, individuals who had only interacted with each other through the prism of war found themselves living and working together as equals. As they listened to each other during rehearsals and discussions, they traversed deep political and ideological divides."[48])

Exercises IV-7A

1. What in-groups are you a member of? Why are you a member of these groups? How do you interact with out-group members? Does being an in-group member cause you any problems with interacting with out-group members?
2. List all the reasons that in-group biases are harmful.
3. List all the reasons that in-group membership is beneficial.
4. Think of situations in the news that involve in-group biases.
5. Think of ways that community-police relationships can be improved by understanding the in-group bias. Look at both sides.
6. How does the in-group bias relate to the bandwagon effect? Do you sometimes adopt a

Biases Concerning Others

position because others in your group hold the same position?
7. Write down five ways an in-group bias might affect your practice.

Exercise IV-7B

How would you overcome the following biases.

1. Fairness in grading tests.
2. Hiring biases.
3. An orchestra is not hiring enough women.
4. A friend from your softball team applies for a job with your company.
5. You are not sure you are treating an applicant from another racial group fairly.

Answers

1. Use anonymous grading.
2. Use algorithms in hiring to double-check your intuitions. (Billy Beane used this method for making personnel decisions when he was GM of the Oakland As.)
3. Blind auditions. (Most orchestras do auditions behind screens.)
4. Have someone else do the hiring.
5. Write down the applicants qualifications and deficiencies, and try to evaluate the applicant objectively. Do a chart for all applicants.

VIII. Curse of Knowledge

One of the worst biases a lawyer can have is the curse of knowledge. The curse of knowledge is "[w]hen better-informed people find it extremely difficult to think about problems from the perspective of lesser-informed people."[49] I hope you can see how much trouble this one can cause a lawyer in dealing with clients, subordinates, and others.

Examples.
Being a poor teacher because you don't understand that your students don't understand a lot of things you do.
Having trouble communicating with your clients because you do not understand what they don't know.
Insulting your clients.
Subordinates making mistakes because you have not explained things to them well-enough.
Insulting subordinates.

Overcoming the Curse of Knowledge

1. Awareness.
2. Consider your audience when explaining things. Don't assume they have the same background knowledge or education as you.

3. Put yourself in your listener's shoes. <u>Educate (teach) your listener or reader.</u>
4. Explain things in detail.
5. Use concrete language.
6. Use simple vocabulary.
7. Give examples.
8. Use stories.
9. Have someone else read your writing for comprehensibility.

Exercise IV-8

1. Take an area you are expert in and think how you would explain it to someone who is new in the field.
2. Practice how you would explain a case to a client. To a judge. To a friend who is not a lawyer.

Wrap Up

Exercises IV-9

Identify the following biases.

1. People from the South all have a funny accent.
2. I don't usually give to charities, but I feel so sorry for that boy who lost his parents in a traffic accident.
3. I support feminism more than my other male friends. (A man is speaking.)
4. He must be good at basketball because he is a Martian.
5. Smith is handsome. He must be smart, too.
6. We Giants fans are much smarter than Jets fans.
7. I prefer to hire women, who like me, went to law school in the 60s. Because there were so few women in law school in the 60s, they are tougher than other groups.
8. I am a Martian who went to college in the 60s. I can understand how Martian college students feel today.
9. I'm going to buy a Honda because all my friends are.
10. I have no trouble handling criticism so I'm tough on my students.
11. Harvard students are much smarter than Yale students. (Speaker goes to Harvard.)
12. AA is the best treatment for all alcoholics.
13. I can be fair to all my students, even though Maggie's parents took me down to their lake house one weekend.
14. It's okay that I take steroids. All college athletes do it.
15. All dogs like Goodie Treats.
16. I favor this candidate. I'm sure my best friend also favors this candidate, even though she hasn't said anything.
17. The witness must be telling the truth. He is a Martian, like me.
18. I'm sure my client has told me the whole truth. He is a successful businessman.

Biases Concerning Others

19. The judge will be disgusted by the defendant's conduct. I know I am.
20. Judge: I don't need to recuse myself from this case even though my wife is a member of the plaintiff class.
21. I don't understand why the client called me. I explained everything in the letter.

Answers

1. Essentialism.
2. Identifiable-victim effect.
3. Possible bias blind spot.
4. Essentialism.
5. Halo effect.
6. In-group bias. Essentialism.
7. In-group bias.
8. Empathy gap.
9. Bandwagon effect.
10. Empathy gap.
11. In-group bias.
12. Essentialism.
13. Bias blind spot.
14. Empathy gap. Bandwagon effect.
15. Essentialism.
16. Projection bias.
17. In-group bias.
18. Halo effect.
19. Projection bias.\
20. Bias blind spot.
21. Curse of knowledge.

Understanding and Overcoming Cognitive Biases for Lawyers and Law Students

Notes

1. *Wikipedia: List of Cognitive Biases.* [https://en.wikipedia.org/wiki/List_of_cognitive_biases]

2. *Id.*

3. Erin Long-Crowell, *The Halo Effect: Definition, Advantages & Disadvantages.* [http://study.com/academy/lesson/the-halo-effect-definition-advantages-disadvantages.html]

4. *Id.*

5. *Id.*

6. Daniel Kahneman, Thinking, Fast and Slow 85 (2011).

7. *Id.*

8. *Id.* at 84-5.

9. *Wikipedia: List of Cognitive Biases.*

10. Romeo Vittelli, *Riding the Bandwagon Effect*, Psychology Today (December 30, 2015) [https://www.psychologytoday.com/blog/media-spotlight/201512/riding-the-bandwagon-effect]

11. Mohammed Ali, *Psychology of bandwagon effect and other cognitive biases*, (April 14, 2012). [https://plus.google.com/+MohammedAliNM]

12. *Wikipedia: Bandwagon Effect.* [https://en.wikipedia.org/wiki/Bandwagon_effect]

13. *Wikipedia: List of Cognitive Biases.*

14. Gus Lubin & Shana Lebowitz, *58 cognitive biases that screw up everything we do*, Business Insider (Oct. 29 (2015). [http://www.businessinsider.com/cognitive-biases-2015-10/#affect-heuristic-1]

15. Leaf Van Boven et. al., *Changing Places: A Dual Judgment Model of Empathy Gaps in Emotional Perspective Taking*, 48 Advances in Experimental Social Psychology 118 (2013). [http://wayback.archive.org/web/20161212190811/http://psych.colorado.edu/~vanboven/VanBoven/Publications_files/VanBovenAdvancesVol48.pdf]

16. *Id.* at 119.

17. *Id.* at 120.

18. *Id.* at 128. *See also* George Lowenstein, *Hot-Cold Empathy Gaps and Medical Decision-Making*, 24 Health Psycholgy 849 (2005).

19. Boven, *supra* at 119.

20. *Id.*

21. *Id.*

22. *Id.* at 120.

23. *Id.* at 122-23.

24. *Id.* at 148.

25. *Id.* at 125.

26. *Id.* at 135.

27. Lowenstein, *supra* at 549.

28. *Id.*

29. *Wikipedia: List of Cognitive Biases.*

30. Shila Rea, *Researchers Find Everyone has a Bias Blind Spot*, Carnegie Melon University (June 8, 2015). [https://www.cmu.edu/news/stories/archives/2015/june/bias-blind-spot.html]

31. Richard F. West et.al., *Cognitive Sophistication Does Not Attenuate the Bias Blind Spot*, 103 Journal of Personality and Social Psychology 506, 507 (2012). [http://keithstanovich.com/Site/Research_on_Reasoning_files/West_Stanovich_JPSP2012.pdf]

32. *Wikipedia: Bias-Blind Spot.* [https://en.wikipedia.org/wiki/Bias_blind_spot]

33. Emily Pronin & Matthew B Kugler, *Valuing thoughts, ignoring behavior: The introspection illusion as a source of the bias blind spot*, 43 Journal of Experimental Social Psychology 565 (2007). [http://www.sciencedirect.com/science/article/pii/S0022103106000916]

34. Alexander Genevsky et.al., Neural Underpinnings of the Identifiable Victim Effect: Affect Shifts Preferences for Giving, 33 J Neurosci. 17188 (2013). [https://www.ncbi.nlm.nih.gov/pmc/articles/PMC3807035/]

35. Elizabeth Chung, *The Identifiable Victim Effect: When One is More Than Many*. [https://www.classy.org/blog/the-identifiable-victim-effect-when-one-is-more-than-.many/]

36. *Id.*

37. Gerald Guild, *Essentailism.* [http://geraldguild.com/blog/2010/03/12/essentialism/comment-page-1/]

38. Susan A. Gelman, *Essentialism in Everyday Thought*, Psychological Science Agenda (May 2005). [http://www.apa.org/science/about/psa/2005/05/gelman.aspx]

39. Guild, *supra.*

40. Maryilynn B. Brewer, *The Psychology of Prejudice: Ingroup Love or Outgroup Hate?*, 55 Journal of Social Issues, 429, 438 (1999). [http://citeseerx.ist.psu.edu/viewdoc/download?doi=10.1.1.197.4614&rep=rep1&type=pdf]

41. *Id.* at 429.

42. *Id.* at 431.

43. *Id.* at 432.

44. *Id.* at 437.

45. *Id.* at 433.

46. *Id.* at 435-36.

47. *Wikipedia: In-Group Favoritism.* [https://en.wikipedia.org/wiki/In-group_favoritism]

48. [http://www.west-eastern-divan.org/]

49. *Wikipedia: List of Cognitive Biases.* [https://en.wikipedia.org/wiki/List_of_cognitive_biases];

Chapter Five
Behavioral Economic Biases

<u>Chapter Goals</u>.
1. To discuss behavioral economic biases in detail.
2. To give the reader ways to deal with behavioral economic biases.
3. To examine the dangers of behavioral economic biases.
4. To show the differences between statistics and expert intuition.

Understanding economics is an important part of being a lawyer. If a lawyer follows a faulty economic model, that lawyer will have great difficulty in being a successful practitioner. The model taught in traditional law and economics classes is faulty because it doesn't account for cognitive biases.

Traditional economic theory (utility theory) is based on the proposition that people are rational actors; they will choose the outcome that has the highest economic payoff. Rational actors are selfish, indifferent to references points and emotions, and indifferent to which deal they take as long as it has the same value. Under traditional economic theory, an item will end up in the hands of the person who values it most from a purely economic viewpoint.

Beginning in the 1970s, a group of economists, including Daniel Kahneman, began to challenge traditional economic theory. They observed that humans are not always selfish and frequently didn't act rationally–that they possess System 1s. Based on these observations, they developed what became known as behavioral economics, prospect theory, or bounded rationality.

They did an experiment where there were two choices:[1]
a. Accept a 50% chance to win a $100, or
b. Accept a 100% chance to win $46

A person under traditional theory would accept the 50% chance of winning $100. Choice a is worth $50 (100 x 50%=50). Choice b is worth $46 (46 x 100%=46). A rational thinker is indifferent to the risk in choice a.

However, under the experiment, most people opted for b, which had less value, but was a safer choice. This showed that humans are not always rational thinkers, and this has been confirmed many, many times. Under behavioral economics, "people's choices are based not on dollar values, but on the psychological value of their outcomes..."[2]

Another part of prospect theory is that the reference point (where you start from) is important.[3] A person who starts with $100 will value a gain of $100 more than a person who starts with $1,000. (Under utility theory, the reference point is not important.)

Examples of Reference Points.[4]
1. The status quo.
2. Par at golf.
3. The negotiated terms of a contract.
4. An animal's territory.
5. Our current rent.
6. Our current salary.
7. A company's profits.

8. A goal. "Not achieving a goal is a loss, exceeding the goal is a gain."

The reference point can change. "The boundary between good and bad is a reference point that changes over time and depends on the circumstances."[5]

Here are some behavioral economic biases:

1. Anchoring effect: "The tendency to rely too heavily, or 'anchor', on one trait or piece of information when making decisions (usually the first piece of information that we acquire on that subject)."
2. Availability heuristic: "The tendency to overestimate the likelihood of events with greater 'availability' in memory, which can be influenced by how recent the memories are or how unusual or emotionally charged they may be."
3. Base-rate effect: "The tendency to ignore base rate information (generic, general information) and focus on specific information (information only pertaining to a certain case)."
4. Endowment effect: "The fact that people often demand much more to give up an object than they would be willing to pay to acquire it."
5. Framing effect: "Drawing different conclusions from the same information, depending on how that information is presented."
6. Gambler's fallacy: "The tendency to think that future probabilities are altered by past events, when in reality they are unchanged."
7. Hyperbolic discounting: "The tendency for people to have a stronger preference for more immediate payoffs relative to later payoffs."
8. Loss aversion: "The disutility of giving up an object is greater than the utility associated with acquiring it."
9. Reactive devaluation: "Devaluing proposals only because they purportedly originated with an adversary."
10. Sunken-cost fallacy: "A cost that has already been incurred and cannot be recovered."[6]

I. Anchoring Effect

Anchoring: "The tendency to rely too heavily, or 'anchor', on one trait or piece of information when making decisions (usually the first piece of information that we acquire on that subject)."[7] "It occurs when people consider a particular value for an unknown quantity before estimating that quantity."[8] In other words, anchoring gives you a reference point, even if that reference point is faulty or irrelevant. Even random numbers can serve as an anchor.[9]

Examples.
Marking up the price of a suit, then putting it on sale. The sale price seems reasonable even if it isn't. (Price tags and the manufacturer's suggested retail price for cars are classic anchors.)
Having a high list price for a house. This helps raise the offers.
Having one or two things on a restaurant menu highly-priced. This makes the other items look reasonable.
Rationing makes people pay higher prices for goods.

Behavioral Economic Biases

Making a medical diagnosis based on the first symptom observed or the first theory considered. An airline cancels your 11 am flight then offers to rebook you on the 4 pm flight. Then, they suddenly discover one extra seat on the 2 pm flight. Your anger about the cancellation goes away.

Legal Examples.
Plea bargaining in a trial. The defendant doesn't want to go to jail at all. The prosecutor offers a long jail term. Later, the prosecutor offers a shorter term. The defendant accepts.
Capping accident awards. Not only does this limit the maximum recoverable, it pulls down awards on all levels.[10] For example, a jury might award a plaintiff $500,000 when there is no cap. When a cap serves as an anchor of $1,000,000, the same jury might award the plaintiff $250,000.

Because of the anchoring effect, it is best to start the negotiations when you are negotiating your salary at a new job.[11]

Possible causes.
1. "[T]he tendency to look for confirmation of things we are not sure of."[12]
2. "A range of uncertainty."[13]
3. Suggestion serves as "'a priming effect,' which selectively evokes compatible evidence."[14]

Many researchers believe that anchoring is hard to avoid.[15] Even being aware of anchoring may help little.[16]

Overcoming the Anchor Bias

1. Getting all the information.
2. Thinking about other comparisons, references, and options.[17]
3. Become an expert in the area.[18] People experienced in an area are less likely to be influenced by an anchor.[19]

Exercises V-1

1. Think of times you have been affected by the anchor effect. Consider how it influenced your decision-making process.
2. Think of ways you can avoid the anchoring effect in a negotiation. Buying a car. Buying a house. Representing a client in a complex real estate deal. Does getting more information help?
3. Is this good or bad? "Last year, accidental deaths during snipe hunting increased 100%."
4. "When I was a kid a soda only cost a dime." Comment.
5. "Look at that motorcycle over there. It's $10,000. This motorcycle isn't as good, but it only costs $5.000." Comment.
6. "Wow, this suit is 60% off list." Comment.
7. "Our ice cream is low in fat and calories." Comment.

8. Think about how cars are usually sold (priced).
9. Do you ever order the special at a restaurant because it sounds better than the regular items? Would you have ordered the special if it had been on the regular menu?
10. Has the anchoring effect ever influenced how you negotiated settlements?
11. Have you ever made a snap analysis of a case because of the first information you received?
12. Has the anchoring effect ever influenced how you plea bargained?
13. Has the anchoring effect ever influenced how one of your clients made a decision?

Comments

3. Sounds bad to me. But what if the accidental deaths went from one to two? Are there any other facts you would like to know? What is the population of the area being surveyed? How many people snipe hunt? To avoid the anchoring effect get all the facts.
4. Meaningless. The price of everything has gone up since she was a kid.
5. The store is using a higher priced item to try to get you to think the lower priced item is a bargain.
6. I wonder if it was ever listed for full price.
7. Yes, but the preservatives cause cancer in laboratory rats. Make sure you get all the information.

II. Availability Heuristic

Availability heuristic: "The tendency to overestimate the likelihood of events with greater 'availability' in memory, which can be influenced by how recent the memories are or how unusual or emotionally charged they may be."[20] Stated more simply, it "is a mental shortcut that relies on immediate examples that come to mind."[21] "When you are trying to make a decision, a number of related events or situations might immediately spring to the forefront of your thoughts. As a result, you might judge that those events are more frequent and possible than others. You give greater credence to this information and tend to overestimate the probability and likelihood of similar things happening in the future."[22]

Professor Kahneman gives a good example of the availability heuristic:

> I recently came to doubt my long-held impression that adultery is more common among politicians than among physicians or lawyers. I had even come up with an explanation for that 'fact,' including the aphrodisiac effect of power and the temptations of life away from home. I eventually realized that the transgressions of politicians are much more likely to be reported than the transgressions of doctors or lawyers. My intuitive impression could be due entirely to journalists' choices of topics and to my reliance on the availability heuristic.[23]

Similarly, after the Love Canal environmental disaster, Congress passed a comprehensive law, CERCLA, which required the clean up of toxic waste sites.[24] Some experts, however, have questioned whether the money might have been spent better elsewhere. The point is that the availability heuristic (the publicity about the disaster) caused environmentalists to focus on toxic waste dumps without fully thinking through other environmental problems.

Examples.
The recent rise in terrorist attacks causes a person to overestimate the possibility she will be in a terrorist attack.
A person who is not in an at risk group worries about getting HIV.
A person is more likely to be in a car accident than an airplane crash, but people are often scared to fly because of the newsworthiness of airplane crashes.
Overestimating your chances of winning the lottery because lottery winners are often mentioned on the news.
Parents fearing that their child will be abducted because of several recent news stories.
People think there are more home foreclosures than there really are because they often appear in the news.
People judge their risk of heart attack by the frequency of heart attacks in their acquittances.

Legal Examples.
People think that more cases go to trial than actually do.
Clients think you can get them a big settlement in their case because they read about big settlements in other cases.

Obviously, some of the examples above are partially based on emotion or the vividness of the event. Emotional or vivid events, such as disasters or terrorist attacks, are etched into our memories, even if their occurrences are rare. Kahneman calls this the "overweighting of unlikely outcomes" or "decision weights."[25] These occur because "[t]he emotional arousal is associative, automatic, and uncontrolled, and it produces a strong impulse for protective action."[26] They are also affected by "[wrongly] focused attention, confirmation bias, and cognitive ease."[27]

Based on the above, it is obvious that a danger of the availability heuristic is the misallocation of resources. For example, a community might allot funds to prevent one disease when another disease is actually more dangerous.

Possible causes.
1. Ease of retrieval.
2. The affect heuristic (emotions). People focus too much on bad events that are in the news, such as airplane disasters.
3. Evolution. In primitive times, humans had to react quickly or be eaten.

Like many heuristics, the availability heuristic substitutes a hard question for an easier one: "you wish to estimate the size of a category for the frequency of the event, but you report an impression of the ease with which instances come to mind."[28]

Understanding and Overcoming Cognitive Biases for Lawyers and Law Students

Overcoming the Availability Heuristic

1. Look at the statistics rather than relying on a snap judgment.
2. <u>Consider all alternate explanations.</u>
3. Focus on content, rather than ease of retrieval or vividness.[29]

Exercise V-2

1. Think of instances where you have suffered from the availability bias. Can you see why you were mistaken?
2. Which activity should receive more funds–prevention of terrorism or highway safety? (Hint: which one causes more deaths?)
3. Car-jacking has been in the news recently. How likely are you to be car-jacked?
4. Motorcycle accidents have been in the news recently. Are motorcycle accidents increasing?
5. Who is the better baseball player–Hank Aaron or Bryce Harper?
6. Has the availability effect ever influenced how you handled a case?
7. Has the availability heuristic ever caused you problems with clients?
8. Sexual harassment has been in the news a lot recently. Do you think there is more sexual harassment today than there was ten years ago?
9. Some people think that getting injured in an accident is like hitting the lottery. Is this really true? Why do people think this? How can this cause problems for an attorney representing such a client?

III. Base-Rate Effect

Base-rate effect: "The tendency to ignore base-rate information (generic, general information) and focus on specific information (information only pertaining to a certain case)."[30] It often occurs because individuals think that statistics don't apply to a particular situation.[31] It can also occur when one uses the wrong base rate or an incomplete base rate.

In evaluating the probability of an occurrence, two types of information may be available:[32]
1. "Generic information about the frequency of events of that type." (The base rate)
2. "Specific information about the case in question."
Thus, the base-rate fallacy occurs when analysts just focus on no. 2.

Problem.
Caitlyn loves to listen to classical recordings. She especially likes Debussy and Mahler. Which is more likely–Caitlyn plays harp in a professional symphony orchestra or she is a secretary?
Answer: Many people would wrongly answer harpist because they are focusing on the specific. However, under the generic (base rate), she is much more likely to be a secretary. There are only about 200 harp jobs in professional symphony orchestras in this country, while there are millions of secretaries.

Behavioral Economic Biases

Examples.
Only 20% of all applicants get into this college. But my son will surely get in because he is brilliant. The problem here is that only brilliant people apply to selective colleges.
Faith healing heals those who truly believe. Two members of our congregation recovered from cancer. (The problem here is that the two members would also have recovered anyway.[33])
Solacold cures colds in just two weeks. (Most colds last two weeks.)

Here, is a more complicated example from *Wikipedia*:

"In a city of 1 million inhabitants let there be 100 terrorists and 999,900 non-terrorists. To simplify the example, it is assumed that all people present in the city are inhabitants. Thus, the base rate probability of a randomly selected inhabitant of the city being a terrorist is 0.0001, and the base rate probability of that same inhabitant being a non-terrorist is 0.9999. In an attempt to catch the terrorists, the city installs an alarm system with a surveillance camera and automatic facial recognition software.
The software has two failure rates of 1%:
The false negative rate: If the camera scans a terrorist, a bell will ring 99% of the time, and it will fail to ring 1% of the time.
The false positive rate: If the camera scans a non-terrorist, a bell will not ring 99% of the time, but it will ring 1% of the time.
Suppose now that an inhabitant triggers the alarm. What is the chance that the person is a terrorist? In other words, what is $P(T \mid B)$, the probability that a terrorist has been detected given the ringing of the bell? Someone making the 'base rate fallacy' would infer that there is a 99% chance that the detected person is a terrorist. Although the inference seems to make sense, it is actually bad reasoning, and a calculation below will show that the chances he/she is a terrorist are actually near 1%, not near 99%.
The fallacy arises from confusing the natures of two different failure rates. The 'number of non-bells per 100 terrorists' and the 'number of non-terrorists per 100 bells' are unrelated quantities. One does not necessarily equal the other, and they don't even have to be almost equal. To show this, consider what happens if an identical alarm system were set up in a second city with no terrorists at all. As in the first city, the alarm sounds for 1 out of every 100 non-terrorist inhabitants detected, but unlike in the first city, the alarm never sounds for a terrorist. Therefore, 100% of all occasions of the alarm sounding are for non-terrorists, but a false negative rate cannot even be calculated. The 'number of non-terrorists per 100 bells' in that city is 100, yet $P(T \mid B) = 0\%$. There is zero chance that a terrorist has been detected given the ringing of the bell.
Imagine that the first city's entire population of one million people pass in front of the camera. About 99 of the 100 terrorists will trigger the alarm—and so will about 9,999 of the 999,900 non-terrorists. Therefore, about 10,098 people will trigger the alarm, among which about 99 will be terrorists. So, the probability that a person triggering the alarm actually is a terrorist, is only about 99 in 10,098, which is less than 1%, and very, very far below our initial guess of 99%.
The base rate fallacy is so misleading in this example because there are many more non-terrorists than terrorists, and the number of false positives (non-terrorists scanned as

terrorists) is so much larger than the true positives (the real number of terrorists)."[34]

In other words, in complicated cases, avoiding the base-rate fallacy requires a lot of math. But, paying attention to this fallacy can help you avoid many reasoning errors.

Overcoming the Base-Rate Effect

1. Use all relevant information.
2. Differentiate the generic from the specific. Understand how these affect a particular evaluation.
3. Think like a statistician. "Your beliefs should be constrained by the logic of probability."[35]

Exercises V-3

1. Consider how the base-rate effect has influenced your thinking.
2. Why is it difficult to focus on the general? Are any other biases at work here?
3. Has the base-rate fallacy ever affected how you drew up a settlement proposal? Has the base-rate fallacy ever influenced how you negotiated a plea bargain?

IV. Endowment Effect

Endowment effect: "The fact that people often demand much more to give up an object than they would be willing to pay to acquire it."[36] This is the bias that most challenges classic economic theory. Under the classic theory, buyers and sellers are rational actors. However, under the endowment effect, people value things they own more than they would value the same item on the open market. Ownership is the reference point.[37] This frequently occurs even if the individual just acquired the item.[38] In other words, humans are often irrational actors in this situation.[39]

Obviously, the endowment effect can interfere with the effectiveness of markets. For example a developer wants to build a shopping center on a parcel of land. The area needs a shopping center, and the land owner can easily buy a similar piece of land for the same price. The buyer wants to pay fair market value. However, the seller wants more because of the endowment effect. Thus, the endowment effect can cause an efficient transaction to fail.

This also applies to governmental takings. When a city buys real estate for a public use, they are supposed to pay fair market value. However, this payment may clash with the endowment effect. Some scholars have suggested that the endowment effect complicates social welfare decisions because it makes determining the cost-benefit of a reallocation difficult.[40]

Of course, not every exchange is subject to the endowment effect. The endowment effect does not occur when items are held "for exchange"–intended to be traded for money or other good.[41] For example, an antiques dealer does not suffer from the endowment effect when he sells a valuable cabinet to a customer.

Examples.
How much an individual would want for her house.

Behavioral Economic Biases

How much a person would want for her grandmother's wedding ring.
"Waterfowl hunters would not pay more than $247, on average, for hunting rights, but also would not sell those rights or anything less than $1044, on average."[42]
Free trials to get people to buy things.

Legal Example.
A lawyer would offer to settle a torts case for $15,000, but would award $10,000 to the aggrieved party as a mediator. Can you see why?

Possible causes.
1. The role of personal wealth in the valuation process.
2. Loss aversion.
3. Sense of possession.

According to Kahneman, "selling goods one would normally use activates regions of the brain that are associated with disgust and pain."[43]

Professors Jones & Brosnan reject the above possibilities and, instead, focus on an evolutionary cause.[44] These authors believe that "evolutionary processes have inevitably influenced (though generally not determined, an important distinction) various human behavioral predispositions by affecting the structure and operations of the human nervous system, including its most significant feature, the brain."[45] More specifically, human brains evolved in a way that aided survival in the past, and these survival mechanisms (behaviors) still affect modern humans.[46] These rational behaviors in the past cause humans irrational behaviors, such as the endowment effect, today (time-shifted rationality). These mechanisms are algorithms–if-then propositions.[47] If a tiger attacks–run.[48] So, "endowment effects might be the results of adaptations to conditions in which the probable results of continued possession were less risky than the probable results of attempted exchanges."[49]

Possible Solutions for the Endowment Effect

1. Awareness. Public policy makers, in particular, need to be aware of how the endowment effect affects transactions.
2. Try to rely on System 2. Ask yourself, if I didn't own this, how much would I pay for it?
3. Rely on a friend's advice when selling items.

Exercises V-4

1. Have you ever felt the endowment effect? Have you tried to sell an item, but the buyer wouldn't pay your price? Was this due to the endowment effect on you?
2. You are selling your house. You receive an offer of $100,000. You feel the price is much too low. Your real estate agent advises you that this is a good price. You wonder if he just wants to get his commission now. What can you do?
3. Have you ever had a problem negotiating a settlement because your client suffered from the

endowment effect?
4. How might the endowment effect influence public takings of private property, such as a residence?

Answers

2. A buyer is generally not going to compensate you for the endowment effect. This means you may not be able to sell your house if you are holding out for a higher price. One way to see if you are being affected by the endowment effect is to ask a friend who has some expertise in real estate for advice. You could also have a professional estimate the fair market value of the house.

V. The Framing Effect

The framing effect is extremely important for lawyers. It affects how a lawyer strategizes a case. Equally important, a lawyer must be aware of how the otherside has framed a case or a negotiation.

Framing effect: "Drawing different conclusions from the same information, depending on how that information is presented." In other words, "manipulating the way information is presented can influence and alter decision making and judgement about that information."[50] Context is the key; "The context in which information is delivered shapes assumptions and perceptions about that information."[51] The frame is the reference point. Our choices are often "'frame-bound' rather than 'reality-bound.'"[52]

Emotions influence the framing effect. Positive frames, which create positive emotions, engender proactive behavior and risk taking, while negative frames produce reactive behavior and risk aversion.[53]

There are three types of framing:[54]
1. <u>Attribute-framing effects</u>: "Attribute-framing effects occur when evaluations of an object or event are more favorable if a key attribute is framed in positive rather than negative terms such as % lean rather than % fat of a food product, % correct rather than % incorrect on a test, and success rate rather than failure rate of a medical procedure."
2. <u>Goal-framing effects</u>: "Goal-framing effects occur when a persuasive message has different appeal depending on whether it stresses the positive consequences of performing an act to achieve a particular goal or the negative consequences of not performing the act."
3. <u>Risky choice-framing effects</u>: "Risky choice-framing effects occur when willingness to take a risk (e.g., elect a medical procedure with variable potential outcomes) depends on whether the potential outcomes are positively framed (e.g., in terms of success rate) or negatively framed (e.g., in terms of failure rate)."

Examples.
The glass is half full. v. The glass is half empty.
A tax v. a user's fee.
"PhD students registered early when the framing was in terms of a penalty fee for late

registration, with only 67% registering early when the framing was in terms of a discount for earlier registration."[55]

How opposing candidates present the same issues or facts.

Candidate A presents himself positively and his opponent negatively.

My opponent missed ten key votes in the Senate this term. v. Senator Sanchez voted 99% of the time this term in the Senate.

'[P]retrial detention may increase a defendant's willingness to accept a plea bargain, since imprisonment, rather than freedom, will be his baseline, and pleading guilty will be viewed as an event that will cause his earlier release rather than as an event that will put him in prison."[56]

98% of our car customers are very satisfied with our vehicle. (Yes, but the other 2% died in fiery crashes caused by defective brkaes.)

The outcome of political polls is often different based on how the question is framed.

    A. Do you support President Trump's policy of temporarily banning immigrants from countries that produce terrorists?

    B. Should the United States accept refugees from war-torn countries?

(Analyze how and why the different frames might produce different results.)

Legal Examples.

How you frame an issue in a brief. You want the judge to accept your presentation of the issue–your framing.

How you frame the outline of a negotiation.

<u>A lot of legal persuaion is about framing.</u>

Possible causes.
1. Emotions
2. Relying too much on System 1.

Overcoming the Framing Effect

1. Try to restate the problem differently. Turn a positive context into a negative one or a negative context into a positive one. ("Framing reversals")[57] Frame the question objectively (neutrally). Make sure you understand the real problem you are dealing with.
2. "When people are exposed to multiple and conflicting frames it causes cognitive dissonance and the framing effect is reduced and neutralized leaving people to rely more on their own internal frames that have been created over time."[58]
3. Consider all the possibilities. Analyze the problem logically. Do the problem on paper so you won't miss any of the alternatives.
4. Combine the possibilities so that you can see the bigger picture. "When you see cases in isolation you are likely to be guided by an emotional reaction of System 1."[59]
5. According to Kahneman costs are not perceived as losses in System 1, so reframe losses as costs.[60] (Obviously, this one creates the possibility of deception.)

Loaded Words

Understanding and Overcoming Cognitive Biases for Lawyers and Law Students

Some people (advertisers, lawyers, politicians) use loaded words–words that have an emotional connotation–to help frame their pitches. For example, in a brief arguing that a defendant's confession was coerced, an attorney might write, "The policeman slammed the suspect against the police car during the arrest." The purpose of the loaded word–slammed–is to active the reader's System 1.

Examples.
During the 1988 presidential election, George Bush labeled his opponent, Michael Dukakis, a card-carrying liberal.
Our facial tissue is soft. (Soft is the loaded word. Loaded words can be positive.)
My opponent is irrational about gun control.
Elbonia is part of the Evil Axis.
The cop slammed the defendant against the police car. v. The cop pushed the defendant against the police car.

When reading, always look for emotional words. Is the word's emotional connotation justified? What is the objective meaning of the word? Is the writer trying to manipulate me? In evaluating an argument always try to evaluate it objectively, and do not let the writer manipulate your System 1 with loaded words.

Sequencing

Sequencing, the order in which items are presented, may also have a framing effect. "[T]he current exposure in the sequence may have the most effect on consumer evaluation judgments due to its recency in memory. That is, the knowledge available to form judgments is strongly influenced by the information in the current advertisement. This notion is consistent with research on memory schemata which indicates that an activated schema (a mind set) can strongly influence how information is processed."[61]

Items that are presented first and last tend to stick in our memories. How does this fact relate to other cognitive biases?

Items presented first can affect how later items are perceived. Example: scores in a gymnastics competition. An early low score can pull down all scores.

Legal writing professors always tell their students to present their side of the case first, then give the facts that are bad for the client. By giving the positive first, the attorney gets the listener on the client's side, which will make the bad facts seem less bad.

Examples.
The order of items on a meeting agenda.
The order legislation is presented for a vote.
The order a company rolls out its ads.
Athletic competitions.

Exercises V-5A

Behavioral Economic Biases

1. Think of when the framing effect has influenced your decisions? Did you jump to a conclusion too quickly without considering the alternatives?
2. Which plan is better–one that produces a 91% employment rate or one that produces 9% unemployment?
3. You are in charge of a marketing campaign for toothpaste. Write an ad for your product. Did you frame the ad in positive or negative terms?
4. Write down at least five examples of the framing effect you have recently seen on television or in the news.
5. Think up examples of the subtypes of the framing effect. Can you articulate the differences among the subtypes?
6. Watch advertisements on television; can you spot the loaded words? Listen to a political speech; can you spot the loaded words?
7. When interviewing for a job, is it better to go first or last?
8. Can you see why framing is vital in litigation?
9. Is it ethical for an attorney to frame a plea-bargaining offer so his client will take it if the lawyer thinks that is the best he can get for the client?
10. Can you see why setting the agenda for a negotiation is important?
11. In settlement negotiations, is it better to make the first offer, or is it better to wait for the otherside to make the first offer.
12. Why do courts throw out eyewitness testimony that was procured under suggestive circumstances?

Answers

2. If you relied on System 1, you probably choose the first alternative. If you did the problem more slowly, you would see that both plans produce the same result.
7. According to one article, "The first candidate to interview might benefit from a committee's primacy bias. The last candidate to interview might benefit from a recency bias."[62] "If it was a good day with many good candidates, it's really a bad idea to be the last," Simonsohn told NPR. "But if it was a weak day with many bad candidates, it's a really good idea to go last." "Some career experts claim there's a recency bias because the latter candidates are fresh in the minds of the committee and there's no reference point for the first evaluation." "If interviewers must judge a large amount of information quickly, they don't have time to make step-by-step evaluations and they reserve their decision to the end." "In that case," Sheehan writes, "the most recent information seems to be the best, and a bias effect occurs toward the most recent interviews in judgment and possibly the most recent candidates interviewed." However, "when the interview process covers a long period of time, interviewers become mentally fatigued and rely on their first impression of a given candidate and tend to choose the applicants interviewed earlier in the process." Finally, "interviewers engaged in 'narrow bracketing,' in which evaluators are reluctant to give a high score to a candidate who followed consecutive candidates who also received high scores."

So, the answer is it is really hard to say for sure. However, if you thoroughly considered this problem in detail, you understand a lot about sequencing.
12. Because the suggestive circumstances influence the framing of the witness's perception.

Understanding and Overcoming Cognitive Biases for Lawyers and Law Students

People often frame questions to get the answers they want. Lawyers do it at a trial; advertisers do it in their ads. Do you see any ethical problems in this?

Exercise V-5B

Reframe the following so they are more likely to be accepted.

1. This product contains 10% fat.
2. The morality rate for this operation is 5%.
3. 10% of our cars go to the junk yard after five years.
4. Our life insurance costs $730 a year.
5. Employee: Can I eat while I'm finishing the project? Boss: No, eating will distract you.
6. A person traveled to Italy when the lira was the currency. A soda was 600 lira. He said, "I'm not paying 600 lira for a soda."
7. An orchestra wants to encourage their patrons to subscribe early. "A subscription to our five concert series is $200. You get a $10 discount if you subscribe before September 1."
8. Our car is the most expensive car on the market.
9. In our lottery game, a winner gets a 50% chance to win $19 on a $10 bet.
10. You will like our tissue better than the other brand.
11. "You should rule that my client is not liable for the plaintiff's injuries. Yes, he was talking on his cell phone at the time of the accident. Yes, his license had expired. Yes, he had stayed up late the night before. But, the accident was caused by the plaintiff driving through a red light."

Answers

1. This product is 90% fat free.
2. 95 % of patients will be saved by this operation.
3. 90% of our cars are still on the road after five years.
4. Our insurance only costs two dollars a day.
5. Employee: Do you mind if I work on the project while I'm eating my lunch? Boss: Sure. I never mind when you work through lunch.
6. A soda in Italy costs $1.
7. A subscription to our five concert series is $190. There is a $10 penalty if you subscribe after September 1. In this example, a gain is changed to a loss.
8. Our car is the most luxurious on the market.
9. In our lottery game, a winner gets a 50% chance to win $19 on a $9 bet. There is a $1 transaction fee on all bets.
10. You will like our tissue better because it is softer than the other brand.
11. "You should rule the my client is not liable for the plaintiff's injuries. The accident was caused by the plaintiff driving through the red light. Everything else my client did is irrelevant because those things did not cause the accident."

Exercise V-5C

Behavioral Economic Biases

1. Reframe the following polling questions to try to change the results.

A. Do you support the President's plan to increase defense spending?
B. Do you support Proposition H, which increases funding for our schools.
C. Do you support the President's plan to prevent terrorists from entering the country?
D. Do you support the Dean's plan to increase the faculty work load?
E. Do you support the President's plan for revenue enhancement?
F. Do you want to hold the prom at the best hotel downtown?

Answers

(There are a lot of possibilities here.)

A. Do support the President's plan to increase military spending by using the social security trust fund?
B. Do you support Proposition H, which increases property taxes 10%.
C. Do you support the President's plan to prevent religious minorities from entering the country?
D. Do you support the Dean's plan to decrease class sizes?
E. Do you support the President's tax increase?
F. Do you want to pay twice as much for your prom ticket, or should we hold it in our school gym?

Be honest. How often are you manipulated by superficial framing?

Finally, you need to be careful in how you phrase questions. Make sure you are not unconsciously framing questions to get the answer you want, unless you are trying to be persuasive.

VI. Gambler's Fallacy

Are lawyers gamblers? Gambler's fallacy: "The tendency to think that future probabilities are altered by past events, when in reality they are unchanged." Stated differently, it "is the mistaken belief that, if something happens more frequently than normal during some period, it will happen less frequently in the future, or that, if something happens less frequently than normal during some period, it will happen more frequently in the future (presumably as a means of balancing nature). In situations where what is being observed is truly random (i.e., independent trials of a random process), this belief, though appealing to the human mind, is false."[63]

The gambler's fallacy requires that the past and future events be independent.[64] For example, when you draw an ace from the deck, this affects the probability you will draw another ace. Another example is if the roulette wheel really is unbalanced.

The gambler's fallacy is similar to the hot-hand fallacy where a person assumes that a hot hand will continue.[65] Kahneman has observed, "The tendency to see patterns in randomness is overwhelming."[66] For example, a coach will keep a basketball player in the game because he is on a shooting streak. A gambler continues to play because she has a hot hand. An investor stays in the stock market. I hope you can see how dangerous this fallacy is.

Examples.
A coin comes up heads five times. What is the probability it will come up tails next time? 50-50. The past coin tosses don't affect the fact that the possibility of a coin coming up tails is always 50%.
Any type of luck against the house at gambling. Since the house takes a cut, the house will win in the long run.

Possible causes.
1. Not understanding the law of small numbers–that small samples represent a larger sample. That five tosses of a coin represents the probability of the next coin toss. Streaks eventually even out.
2. There is justice in the world. There is some power that affects random events.
3. A person's luck can influence the outcome.
4. "Functional magnetic resonance imaging has revealed that, after losing a bet or gamble ("riskloss"), the frontoparietal network of the brain is activated, resulting in more risk-taking behavior. In contrast, there is decreased activity in the amygdala, caudate, and ventral striatum after a riskloss. Activation in the amygdala is negatively correlated with gambler's fallacy—the more activity exhibited in the amygdala, the less likely an individual is to fall prey to the gambler's fallacy. These results suggest that gambler's fallacy relies more on the prefrontal cortex (responsible for executive, goal-directed processes) and less on the brain areas that control affective decision-making."[67]

Overcoming the Gambler's Fallacy

1. Learn the laws of probability.
2. Determine whether a present event can be influenced by a particular past event. Check for a causal connection.
3. Watch out for the gambler's fallacy in things that don't seem to be gambles on the surface. (planning for disasters)

Exercises V-6

1. Think of instances where you have suffered from the gambler's fallacy. Why did you connect past events with unrelated future events?
2. Think of instances of the gambler's fallacy in the business world.
3. Have you ever suffered from the gambler's fallacy when negotiating a settlement?
4. Attorney: I have won 90% of my cases. I have a 90% chance of winning your case. Is this an example of the gambler's fallacy?

Answer

4. Probably not. If the attorney has a long-track record, her success may be due to her ability as an attorney. The answer is simplistic; though, other factors may affect the outcome of this case. The case may be unwinnable. There may be an overconfidence effect here.

VII. Hyperbolic Discounting

Hyperbolic discounting: "The tendency for people to have a stronger preference for more immediate payoffs relative to later payoffs." An example of hyperbolic discounting is when a person prefers $5 now against $10 in a month.[68]

Economists use a discounted utility approach to consider the effect of time on choices.[69] Because consequences are delayed with intertemporal choices, the analyst must discount them (reweigh).[70] Theoretically, humans should be using an exponential discounting model, which is time-consistent model of discounting.[71] However, studies have shown that humans often do not act in a rational manner and use the exponential discount model, but instead adopt the time-inconsistent model of hyperbolic discounting.[72] For example, under an exponential model, an individual would want to be compensated with market interest to compensate for the delay in receiving money. However, under a hyperbolic-discounting model, a person would take the money now, rather than waiting for a higher payoff in the future.

Examples.
Selling a house now for a lower price instead of a year from now for a higher price.
Substance abuse. Fun tonight, hangover tomorrow. Fun now, addiction later.
We can worry about global warming later.
Credit cards. I know I can't afford those shoes, but I won't have to pay for them now if I put them on my credit card.
Buying a car now, rather than waiting for a sale.
Not saving enough for retirement. Live for today.
Procrastination. I want to party today; I'll write the paper tomorrow.

With long-delays in litigation, hyperbolic discounting may affect how you and your client undertake settlement negotiations. Is it better to take $100,000 now or $200,000 in two years?

Possible causes.
1. The brain is wired for present satisfaction.[73]
2. Evolutionary explanation. Kill food now even if better food may be available later. In other words, humans sustained life by getting a little bit now rather than a lot later.[74]
3. Uncertain risks.

Overcoming Hyperbolic Discounting

1. Reframe the problem.
2. Carefully consider all the possibilities.

Exercises V-7

1. Think of instances where you have been guilty of hyperbolic discounting?
2. Would you rather take a vacation today or save for retirement? Think about how you have planned for retirement. Do you have a solid plan, or does it reflect hyperbolic discounting?
3. Has hyperbolic discounting affected how you invest?
4. Do you often suffer from procrastination? How has it affected your life?
5. I am sure you have heard about businesses that will pay you now for a structured settlement. Why do people accept these offers? Is this economically smart?

VIII. Loss Aversion

Loss aversion: "The disutility of giving up an object is greater than the utility associated with acquiring it."[75] In other words, people prefer avoiding a loss over receiving a gain.[76] For example, people would prefer not to lose $1000 over gaining $1000. Loss aversion, psychologically, may be twice as strong as gains.[77] Loss aversion is why many people are risk averse.[78]

Examples.
Staying at a play you don't like because you've already paid for the ticket.
Holding on to falling stocks.
Staying on hold for an hour to get a dollar refund.
Requiring more to give up something than you would pay to buy it.

Like the endowment effect, loss aversion may cause difficulties in settlement negotiations or business transactions.

Possible causes.
1. An evolutionary advantage. "Because a loss of precious resources reads as a threat to our very survival, we're hardwired to try to hold on to what we have."[79]
2. Emotions.

Solutions to Loss Aversion

1. Awareness.
2. Reframe the problem. Change the perspective.

Exercises V-8

1. How has loss aversion affected you? Have you ever felt it in an emotional sense?
2. Your employer offers to give you health benefits in exchange for a 10% reduction in salary. The value of the health benefits is slightly more. Do you take the deal?
3. The county offers you $100,000 for your house so that it can build a new park. Your house is worth $100,000, and the county has offered you pay all your relocation expenses. Do you take the deal?
4. Are you risk averse? Think about what is causing you to be risk averse. Is it better to be

risk averse or risk seeking? Think of some instances where being risk averse is an advantage.
5. How is loss aversion similar to the endowment effect?
6. Has loss aversion ever caused you problems in settling a case?

Part of loss aversion is the weighting of losses.[80] Humans will pay a premium to avoid a loss because of loss aversion. For example, in a choice between a 90% chance of receiving $95 and a 50% chance of receiving $180, most people will choose to receive the $95. This makes no sense under traditional economic theory. The utility of the first choice is $85.5, and the utility of the second is $90. The only explanation for most individuals' irrational choice is that they fear a loss more than they favor a gain.

Interestingly, studies show that a golfer will work harder to avoid a bogey (a loss), than to achieve a birdie (a gain).[81]

Similar to the weighting of losses is the certainty principle–people will pay a premium for a certain outcome.[82] Most people would rather have a 100% chance of receiving $95, than a 98% chance of receiving $100. Most people fear small losses.

Of course, this loss/risk aversion causes real economic losses because people pay more to avoid a loss than a thing or transaction is worth. Kahneman suggests broader framing (combining several transaction, rather than treating each transaction in isolation) to the costs of risk aversion.[83] Broad framing can blunt the emotional reaction to risk.[84]

An example is not buying an extended warranty. Extended warranties are generally bad deals; you pay much more than the protection you receive. In isolation, humans want the protection of an extended warranty. "Oh, it will be a disaster if my computer breaks down." However, if you adopt a broad frame and avoid all extended warranties you will probably be better off. "I will never buy an extended warranty. If something breaks, I'll use the money I didn't use for extended warranties, and I still come out ahead."

Here is another example:[85] You need some cash. Should you sell the stock that has been doing well or the stock that has been losing money? Most people would sell the stock that is doing well because people get pleasure from selling winners. But is this the best decision? No, this is narrow framing. You should sell the stock that is probably going to fall in the future and ignore the past. "A rational decision maker is only interested in the future consequences of current investments."[86]

IX. Reactive Devaluation

This one can really hurt an attorney. Reactive devaluation: "Devaluing proposals only because they purportedly originated with an adversary."[87] Reactive devaluation can be a major impediment to negotiations–both political and business negotiations.[88] (Think Congress)

Examples.
Rejecting a proposal if it comes from a politician you dislike like.
Rejecting a settlement because it comes from a lawyer you dislike.
Voting against a proposal at a faculty meeting that was put forth by someone you dislike.
A newspaper almost always disagrees with everything President Trump says.
Devaluing compromises made by the other side.

Understanding and Overcoming Cognitive Biases for Lawyers and Law Students

A cable network almost always disagreed with everything President Obama said.
"In another study, experimenters showed Israeli participants a peace proposal which had been actually proposed by Israel. If participants were told the proposal came from a Palestinian source they rated it lower than if they were told (correctly) the identical proposal came from the Israeli government. If participants identified as "hawkish" were told it came from "dovish" Israeli government they believed it was relatively bad for their people and good for the other side, but not if participants identified as 'doves.'"[89]

Overcoming Reactive Devaluation

1. Think for yourself.
2. Avoid emotions in evaluations.
3. Don't tell interested parties who came up with the proposal.
4. Employ a mediator.
5. Consult with someone who doesn't know where the idea came from.

Exercises V-9

1. Have you ever disagreed with something because it came from someone you disliked?
2. Can you think of instances where a mediator quickly settled a dispute that had been going on for months?
3. Can you think of instances where you had trouble settling a case because you didn't like the other attorney? How did this affect your client?

X. Sunken-Cost Fallacy

Sunken-cost fallacy: "A cost that has already been incurred and cannot be recovered."[90] It is not knowing when to quit. The sunken cost fallacy focuses on past costs rather than future utility (a backward-looking decision).[91] This is another instance where the past is not connected to the future. Don't let your emotions get in the way.

Examples.
Staying in college after two years, even though you don't like it and don't think it will help your future.
Continuing with a losing investment.
Continuing with a losing romantic relationship.
Eating a bad meal because you've paid for it.
Not selling a junk car because you've already paid a lot to repair it.
Not throwing out old clothes.
Eating too much at a buffet.
You buy a ticket for a movie online. You then read a review of the movie that makes you think you won't like it. You go to the movie anyway.
I bought a ticket to movie A online for $5 dollars. I later bought a ticket to movie B for $10 dollars. To my horror, I discover that both tickets are for the same time. Even though I would

Behavioral Economic Biases

rather go to movie A because it got great reviews, I go to movie B. (Assume this is the last showing of each movie.)

Cost overruns.

The DOD has spent five billion dollars on a new type of bomber that is not particularly effective. It stays with that plane even though there are better bombers available.

Legal Examples.

Continuing with litigation that cannot be won.
Continuing a law firm that cannot be saved.
Staying in law school even when you are doing very poorly because you have already paid one year's tuition.

Possible causes.[92]
1. Loss aversion.
2. Fear of wasting.
3. Reluctance to admit a mistake.
4. Emotions (bad feelings at giving something up). (Don't let regret get in your way,)
5. Failure to see the positive opportunities.
6. To avoid criticism.
7. Framing effects.

Overcoming the Sunken Cost Fallacy

1. A careful cost-benefit analysis without considering the sunken costs.
2. Step outside yourself. How would an objective party view the situation?
3. Objectively consider the alternatives.
4. Allow a margin of error.
5. Don't throw good money after bad.
6. Set budget limits beyond which the company will not spend.
7. Bring in a new management team that is not already invested in the project.

Some researchers believe that the sunken-cost fallacy is good at times because it can force a person to complete a project, which might be ultimately beneficial, they might not finish otherwise.[93] Of course, the key to determining this is to do a cost-benefit analysis.

Exercises V-10

1. Think about times you have suffered from the sunken cost fallacy? Why did you stick with the bad decision?
2. Are you reluctant to throw out things? Why? Do the items have any real worth? Do they have emotional value? Have you ever passed on an opportunity because you were already involved in something else that wasn't working?
3. Have you ever given up on a sunken cost, and it turned out to be the right decision?
4. Are you a good poker player? Do you know when to fold a hand?

5. Have you ever continued with litigation when you knew you were going to lose. How did this make you feel.
6. Has a client ever wanted to continue with litigation when you had informed him he had a losing case. How did you handle this?

XI. Theory-Induced Blindness

Kahneman calls traditional economic theory theory-induced blindness.[94] He states, "If you come upon an observation that does not seem to fit the model, you assume that there must be a perfectly good explanation that you are somehow missing."[95] In other words, if the facts don't fit the theory, it is the facts that are wrong, not the theory. A clear thinker would examine it the other way around, i.e., what is wrong with the theory.

Many intellectuals are guilty of theory-induced blindness. They don't question their theories that have holes or have been disproved completely. Think of those who refused to concede that the earth was not the center of the universe or that man evolved from lower species. This theory-induced blindness is not limited to the past. For example, scientists have definitively proven that vaccines do not cause autism. Yet, some very intelligent people cling to this theory despite the fact that they have nothing to support their theory. They are letting their System 1s control their thinking.

Dilbert cartoons are a great source for examples of theory-induced blindness.

Overcoming Theory-Induced Blindness

1. Don't overly rely on theory. Don't deify theory.
2. If the facts don't match the theory, the theory is probably wrong.

Exercise V-11

1. Think of instances when your thinking has been controlled by theory-induced blindness.
2. Think of instances you've heard on the news of theory-induced blindness.
3. Has theory-induced blindness ever affected how you litigated a case or conducted a negotiation? This one may take a lot of thought, but I bet you have.

XII. Reference-Dependent Fairness

The economic biases we discussed above affect our concepts of fairness. For example, "A basic rule of fairness . . . is that the exploitation of market power to impose losses on others is unacceptable."[96] Say there is a hurricane in a region. A store sold bottle water for $1 before the hurricane, but it sells it for $2 after. Humans consider this unfair, even though it satisfies traditional economic notions of supply and demand. This occurs because the original price is a reference point and the increase in price is a loss to the consumer.

An employee in the fast food industry has a salary of $12 an hour.[97] Wages for similar jobs in the area have gone down to $10 per hour. The employer lowers the worker's salary (an entitlement) to $10 per hour. This is considered an unfair gain because the reference point is

Behavioral Economic Biases

$12 and the worker has incurred a loss. However, this would not be an unfair gain if the employer had lowered the salary because the employer's expenses had gone up. This is not an unfair gain because both parties have an entitlement (salary, existing profits). The employer is not gaining at the worker's expense, but rather is protecting its entitlement. (Of course, Kahneman and his partners confirmed this through experiments.)

Consider the same facts, but with a new employee rather than an existing one. Previously, the employer had paid its workers a salary of $12 an hour. The market salary in the area falls to $10 an hour. The employer gives the new employee $10 per hour. This is fair because the new employee did not have an entitlement; the employee did not suffer a loss.

In sum, traditional economic theory is wrong that fairness is irrelevant to economic behavior and that economic behavior is governed only by self-interest.

Exercise V-12

1. Your rent is $1,000 a month. Market rates for a similar apartment in the area have increased to $1,2000 a month. Is it fair for your landlord to raise your rent to $1,200 a month to match the market rate? What if the landlord has increased the rent to retain its profit margin? What if the landlord charges the new market rate just to new tenants?
2. Two parties entered into a coal supply contract. Company A mines coal, while Company B sells coal to consumers. By the time the contract comes up for renewal, the price of coal in the area has increased $10% because of a shortage. Company A wants Company B to pay it 10% more than the originally-negotiated price. Company B thinks this is unfair. Is it right?
3. Think of examples of reference-dependant fairness you've seen in practice.

Answers

1. You should be able to answer this one based on the examples above.
2. It is not unfair. The price of coal has increased making the pie bigger for both parties. Company B can increase the price to its consumers. There has been no loss here.

XIII. The Dangers of Behavioral Economic Biases

Can you list the dangers of being subject to the behavioral economic biases? Professor Owen Jones has noted that "instead of winding up in the hands of those who value them most, goods and rights will tend to stay in the hands of those into whose hands they first get."[98]

Exercise V-13

Consider all the cognitive biases in this chapter. What are the potential dangers of these biases? In law practice?

XIV. Statistics versus Expert Intuition

Lawyers rely on both intuition (clinical predictions) and statistical analysis (statistical predictions). In general, which is more accurate? When the prediction involves significant uncertainty and unpredictability ("low-validity environments"), the statistical prediction.[99] Numerous studies have shown that, when low-validity environments are involved, "[i]n every case, the accuracy of experts was matched or exceeded by a simple algorithm."[100] This is significant because statistical predictions are usually less expensive than clinical ones.[101]

For example, a statistician developed a formula for predicting the price of fine wines, based on yearly weather variations, which had a correlation of over .90 between his predictions and the prices.[102] How much money could you make if your stock predictions were over 90% accurate?

Why are statistical predications better than clinical predictions in low-validity environments? Answer: the extreme context dependency of System 1. Studies of priming have shown that "unnoticed stimuli in our environment have a substantial influence on our thoughts and actions."[103] In other words, irrelevant information affects clinical predictions, but not statistical ones. So, problem-solvers should check their intuitive predictions with statistical ones. In some cases, it may be cheaper not to do the clinical prediction at all!

Examples.
Admissions decisions for medical school or law school. "[C]onducting an interview is likely to diminish the accuracy of the selection process.... Because interviewers are overconfident in their intuitions..."[104]

Daniel Kahneman's Guide to Interviewing

1. "Select a few traits that are prerequisites for success in this position (technical proficiency, engaging personality, reliability, and so on)." Make the traits as independent as possible.
2. "Make a list of questions for each trait and think about how you will score it on a 1-5 scale." "To avoid halo effects, you must collect the information on one trait at a time before you move on to the next one."
3. Add up the scores. "Firmly resolve that you will hire the candidate whose final score is the highest, even if there is another one you like better."[105]

The above seems counterintuitive, and it may make you uncomfortable. Ironically, this is because of your System 1. However, studies have demonstrated that it is accurate. It is often hard to overcome System 1, but we must do it to become effective thinkers. As proponents of algorithms have argued, "It is unethical to rely on intuitive judgments for important decisions if an algorithm is available that will make fewer mistakes."[106]

Here is what Kahneman said about his study of statistical predictions: "I learned from this finding a lesson that I have never forgotten: intuition adds value even in the justly derided selection interview, but only after a disciplined scoring of objective information and a disciplined scoring of separate traits."[107]

Exercises V-14A

1. Imagine the reactions of clinical predictors when they read the results of the studies on

Behavioral Economic Biases

clinical predictions? Similarly, consider the reactions of scientists and other intellectuals when Galileo proved the earth was not the center of the universe. Think up other instances where scientific discoveries radically changed how humans think. Now, imagine what would have happened if these discoveries would have been rejected.
2. Design a protocol for interviewing a candidate in your field or for your job.
3. Which approach should produce more accurate results for predicting damages in a torts case–intuition or statistical analysis?

More on Expert Intuitions

The above does not question the validity of all expert intuitions. In some cases, expert intuitions can be accurate. There are two types of expert intuitions: 1) intuitions that "draw primarily on skill and expertise acquired by repeated experience" and 2) "heuristics that []substitute an easy question for the harder one that was asked."[108] I have shown the problems with the second type of intuition earlier. However, the first type can be useful because it is based on "skill and expertise acquired by repeated experience."[109] In other words, the expert recognizes familiar cues.[110] In sum, the first type of intuition evaluates evidence, while the second type involves uncertainty. Expert predictions are more accurate when they involve little uncertainty.

For example, chess masters can draw on hundreds of possible moves because they have spent years playing chess. Similarly, doctors who have spent years learning diseases, can intuitively match a patient's symptoms with knowledge stored in long-term memory to make a correct diagnosis.

Acquiring expertise requires years of training to obtain knowledge and develop the ability to recognize cues. It requires quality feedback (formative feedback) and a great deal of practice.[111]

Exercises V-14B

Label the following as type 1 or type 2 intuitions.

1. A lawyer initially evaluates a client's business plan.
2. A basketball player fakes out the defender and scores.
3. An admissions officer interviews college applicants.

Which of the following are likely to be accurate expert predictions and which are not.

4. Long-term financial forecasts.
5. A football coach's defensive strategy.
6. A chess master's moves.
7. A novice checker player's moves.

Go through tasks you frequently perform as a lawyer. Which are better done through intuition and which are better done through statistical analysis?

Understanding and Overcoming Cognitive Biases for Lawyers and Law Students

Answers

1. Type 1. Draws on the lawyer's knowledge.
2. Type 1.
3. Type 2. Uncertainty is involved here.
4. No.
5. Yes.
6. Yes.
7. No. A novice has no cues or knowledge to draw upon.

Experts can take some of the uncertainty out of type 2 predictions by using System 2. For example, intensity matching compares things on two different scales.[112]

Example.
1. John runs the fastest fifty yards in our team.
2. Therefore, he is our best wide receiver.

I hope you see the problem here: it is uncertain whether a fast runner will be a good wide receiver. Speed is important to a receiver, but other factors are also essential.

There is a way to deal with the uncertainty: determine the correlation between the measures, with the correlation being the shared factors.[113] This will help you produce unbiased and moderate predictions rather than extreme ones.
Here is a way to take out the uncertainty:[114]

1. Start with the baseline.
2. Come up with your intuition based on the evidence.
3. Estimate the correlation between the baseline and your intuition. (From System 2)
4. Move the distance from the average to your intuition based on the correlation.

Say you are trying to predict a future law student's gpa. You think that the grade a student earns in Logic is a good predictor of law school success based on your many years of teaching. Joan did well in Logic. You predict that she will be an A- (92) student in law school. Now let's do the math.

1. 80=average law school grade. (The baseline based on statistics)
2. 92=your intuition of Joan's law school gpa.
3. .90=your estimate of the correlation between the baseline and Joan's gpa.
4. 90.8=modified intuition.

Let's change the problem a little, and say the correlation is .30, then the predicted gpa would be 83.6. If it is 0 (no correlation), it would be 80. (In this case, you had no evidence to base your intuition on. Again, you base the correlation on the shared factors between the baseline and the intuition evidence. So, if there are no shared factors, reject your intuition

Behavioral Economic Biases

completely.) If it is 1 (total confidence), it would be 92.

Kahneman observed that his method, "builds on your intuition, but it moderates it, regresses it to the mean. When you have good reason to trust the accuracy of your intuitive prediction–the adjustment will be small."[115] "The corrected intuitive predictions eliminate these biases, so that predictions (both high and low) are about equally likely to overestimate and underestimate the true value."[116] So, with the example, you have used the base rate and considered the quality of the information (your intuition) through the correlation.

Exercise V-14C

1. Write an interview protocol based on this method?

Answer

I know this is really hard. First, find a base rate. This would be the average score for all candidates, based on the statistical scores used above. (ex. 60). Now, have someone interview the candidate who is not aware of the candidates statistical score. (Knowing the statistical score would probably bias the intuition). Say, on a scale of 100, the interviewer gives the candidate an 80. You estimate that the correlation between the base rate and intuition is .50. Therefore the candidate would receive a final score of 70. You can compare the statistical score with the intuition score to select the best candidate.

Wrap Up

Overcoming Behavioral Economic Biases

1. Be aware that these biases exist.
2. Gather all the facts before making a decision.
Restate the problem. Positive to negative. Negative to positive.
3. Don't jump to conclusions. Consider all alternatives. Use System 2.
Do a statistical analysis, when possible.
4. Consult with others.
5. Ask whether you are making a rational decision or an emotional one.
6. Look for a causal connection or a lack of one.
7. Determine whether statistical or clinical analysis will produce the best results.

Exercises V-15A

Identify the following biases.

1. I'm going to get cancer. Three of my friends have it.
2. I'd like to switch to a business major, but I've already spent three years as a history major.
3. The patient must have pneumonia. He is having trouble breathing.
4. The otherside's offer is unacceptable.

Understanding and Overcoming Cognitive Biases for Lawyers and Law Students

5. I paid $500 for that vase last month, but I won't take less than a $1,000 to sell it.
6. As she was growing up, Trisha liked to sculpt. Which is more likely–she is a sculptor or she is a doctor?
7. I know the stock price is falling and the company might go into bankruptcy, but I'm not selling it.
8. The roulette wheel has come up black seven times. I'll bet on black because it will come up black again.
9. I can pay $500 dollars now or make monthly payments of $150 for five months. I will make the payments.
10. This treatment will save 200 lives versus this treatment will save 25% of those with the disease.
11. This dress is a great bargain; it's marked down 50%.
12. The couch costs 50% less at this store, but I won't have to make a payment until next year at the other store.
13. The relator said my house was worth $100,000, but I won't sell it for less than $150,000.
14. I favor tax cuts, but the one proposed by the other party's senator is unreasonable.
15. The trip will cost $500, but there will be a $100 penalty if you pay after May 1. The trip will cost $600, but it will cost $500 if you pay now.
16. My attorney says we can't win the case. However, I don't want to stop because I've already spent $10,000 litigating this case.
17. This is a good location to set up a practice. A couple of my friends have done well in this area.
18. The otherside's offer is unfair. The other attorney stole my girlfriend in law school.
19. My client won't accept the offer because he thinks his house is worth more than that.
20. The other side offered $50,000 to settle, so I think we should counter with 55.

Answers

1. Availability heuristic.
2. Sunken-cost fallacy.
3. Anchoring bias.
4. Reactive devaluation.
5. Loss aversion or endowment effect.
6. Base-rate effect.
7. Sunken-cost fallacy.
8. Gambler's fallacy.
9. Hyperbolic discounting.
10. Framing effect.
11. Anchoring effect.
12. Hyperbolic discounting.
13. Endowment effect or loss aversion.
14. Reactive devaluation.
15. Framing effect.
16. Sunken-cost fallacy.

Behavioral Economic Biases

17. Availability heuristic.
18. Reactive devaluation.
19. Endowment effect.
20. Possible anchoring bias.

Extended Exercises

When you reach a letter, discuss the possible cognitive biases and solutions. (Some of the biases are from earlier chapters.) If you are having trouble, consult the list of cognitive biases in Chapter One.

1. Ad on late night tv.

   For the first time on tv the Miracle Juicer! [A] All your friends are buying one. [B] You would have to pay $29.99 to buy one in a store, but the Miracle Juicer is only $9.95 if you buy one now. [C] And there's more! Call the toll-free number in the next hour, and we will give you a second Miracle Juicer for free. [D] [General comments]

2. Couple meets with a realtor concerning the sale of a house.

   Realtor: The market price for the house is $200,000 so I suggest this as the list price.
   Husband: I don't know. We were hoping for more, like 250. [A]
   Realtor: I don't think we can get that much. It's way above what other properties in the area are selling for.
   Wife: What if we list it for 250 to make others think that a lower price will be a bargain. [B]
   Realtor: If you price it much over 200, you might have to wait a year to sell it.
   Husband [looking at wife]: Okay. [C]
   Realtor: What should the headline be on the ad.
   Wife: How about "quiet neighborhood with lake front view?" [D]
   Realtor: That's good, but it describes most of the houses in the area. [E]
   Husband: Living room with cathedral ceiling, plenty of room for kids. [F]
   Realtor: Sounds good. Families look for houses this time of year.
   Wife: Should we mention the flooding problem in the ad?
   Realtor: No, let's save that for later. Let's let them fall in love with the house first. [G]
   Realtor: What about that separate lot you own on Vine? The appraisal said the property's worth 75.
   Husband: No, no, no. We paid 100 for it two years ago. [H]
   Realtor: I know but the market price for properties has really dropped in that area. I don't think we can get more than 75.
   Husband: List it for 100; we won't take a penny less. [I]
   Realtor: Okay, I'll list it for that, but I think that we will have to eventually lower the price.
   Husband: Then, I'll sell it myself. I know lots of people who are looking for in-

vestment property. [J]

Comments

1.

A. Strong opening that tries to appeal to your emotions.
B. Using the bandwagon effect to reach your emotions.
C. Anchor bias. $9.99 must be a bargain. Overcome this one by pausing for a second. Ask yourself if they are really $29.99 in stores.
D. A type of hyperbolic discounting. The ad is trying to get you to buy now, rather than waiting and seeing if this really is a bargain. Also, related to availability heuristic.
General comments. We see ads like this all the time, but they often work. The ad is appealing to your System 1 emotions. It wants you to make an impulse buy now, rather than slowing down and using your System 2. They don't give you enough information to make a proper decision, but, if you wait, you will start to recognize the problems with the ad.

2.

A. Endowment effect. Because they own the property, the couple rejects market value.
B. The wife wants to use the anchoring effect here. Do you see any problems? [Available buyers might be scared away by the high asking price.]
C. Hyperbolic discounting. I'd rather have my money today.
D. She is framing the ad.
E. I like how the realtor is handling the client. Instead of saying it's a bad idea, she says it's a good idea and offers a better alternative. This will avoid making the wife mad. The realtor is really using her System 2.
F. Framing again.
G. This is a common persuasiveness technique. Give the positive before the negative. She is trying to create an expectation bias. Of course, they will have to reveal all defects in the property at some point.
H. Loss aversion.
I. The husband's attitude shows how strong loss aversion can be. He is suffering from an expectation bias. He is rejecting all information that disagrees with his loss aversion.
J. Overconfidence effect and illusion of control. He can't control the market.

Exercises for Lawyers

Now that you know the most important cognitive biases, do the following exercises.

1. Your client is a well-know celebrity who you have admired for many years. How might this cause you difficulties in your representation?
2. You are representing your client in the dissolution of a partnership. He tells you that he is responsible for the partnership's success and that the other partner did very little. What bias

Behavioral Economic Biases

might be involved here, and how might it affect your representation?

3. The opposing attorney, who you dislike, makes a settlement offer in your case. You advise your client to reject the settlement. Is there a possible bias here?

4. At the initial meeting with your client, you thought that your client was innocent. Since that meeting, new evidence has come out that places doubt on your client's story. However, you still believe your client is innocent. What possible bias might be involved here? How will your continued belief in your client's innocence affect your handling of the case? Could it cause your client problems?

5. No matter what you do, you cannot get your client to understand the contract. What might be the problem here?

6. Your client is sued for employment discrimination. He tells you that he has never discriminated against anyone in his life and that he donates money to liberal charities. What bias might be present here?

7. You are hiring a new secretary. You interview two good candidates–one from your ethnic group and another who is not. You think the one from your ethic group would be the better secretary so you hire him. What cognitive bias might be present?

8. In a previous case, you had problems dealing with an attorney who has now represents someone who has sued one of your clients. What do you need to be careful of?

9. You lost a case because one of your associates failed to find an important case? What do you tell the client? How do you handle the associate?

10. Your client lost her husband in a traffic accident, and you are representing her in a wrongful death case. You are getting tired of your client crying so much whenever you meet. What do you do?

Answers

1. Be aware of the possible presence of the halo effect.

2. Your client may suffer from a self-serving bias. This may cause difficulties in settling the dissolution.

3. Be aware of reactive devaluation. Make sure your are basing your advice on System 2 instead of System 1.

4. Semmelweis reflex. You always want to believe that your client is innocent or is in the right. However, going too far with this can hurt the client. In this example, if the client is guilty, it might be better to plea bargain than to go to trial.

5. The curse of knowledge. You will usually know much more about the law than the client will. Don't expect your client to have the equivalent of a law school education. Explain the case to the client in a manner the client will understand. (However, never be condescending.)

6. Bias blind spot. Be very careful in handling this one. No one likes to be accused of being biased. Rather, show your client how his actions might have violated the law.

7. In-group bias.

8. Emotional reasoning. Make sure you are using your System 2, not your System 1.

9. You need to be careful of unfair blaming. Yes, the associate made a mistake, but you were in charge. If the associate made other mistakes, I would get rid of her, but don't hold the associate completely at fault when you also made a mistake. Sorry, you are going to have to

take responsibility with the client because you were in charge.

10. Realize that you might be suffering from an empathy-gap bias. You do not want to be too emotionally involved with your client's case because this might affect how you handle the case. However, you still need to be empathetic to your clients.

In sum, don't let your System 1 force you to make a choice that is objectively the worse one.

Notes

1. Daniel Kahneman, Thinking, Fast and Slow 271 (2011).

2. *Id.* at 273.

3. *Id.* at 279, 281.

4. *Id.* at 303-09.

5. *Id.* at 302.

6. *Wikipedia: List of Cognitive Biases.* [https://en.wikipedia.org/wiki/List_of_cognitive_biases]

7. *Id.*

8. Kahneman, *supra* at 119.

9. *Wikipedia: Anchoring.* [https://en.wikipedia.org/wiki/Anchoring]

10. Kahneman, *supra* at 127.

11. *Anchoring Effect: How The Mind is Biased by First Impressions,* Psyblog. [http://www.spring.org.uk/2013/05/the-anchoring-effect-how-the-mind-is-biased-by-first-impressions.php]

12. *Id.*

13. Kahneman, *supra* at 121.

14. *Id.* at 123.

15. *Wikipedia: Anchoring.*

16. *Id.*

17. Psyblog, *supra.*

18. *Id.*

19. *Wikipedia: Anchoring.*

20. *Wikipedia: List of Cognitive Biases.*

21. Kendra Cherry, *What is the Availability Heuristic?*, VeryWell (April 26 2016). [https://www.verywell.com/availability-heuristic-2794824].

22. *Id.*

23. Kahneman, *supra* at 7-8.

24. *Id.* at 143.

25. *Id.* at 323.

26. *Id.*

27. *Id.* at 324.

28. *Id.* at 131.

29. *Id.* at 135.

30. *Wikipedia: List of Cognitive Biases.*

31. Logically Fallacious, *Base Rate Fallacy*. [https://www.logicallyfallacious.com/tools/lp/Bo/LogicalFallacies/55/Base_Rate_Fallacy]

32. *The Base Rate Fallacy*, Fallacy Files. [http://www.fallacyfiles.org/baserate.html]

33. Logically Fallacious, *supra*.

34. *Wikipedia: Base Rate Fallacy* [https://en.wikipedia.org/wiki/Base_rate_fallacy]

35. Kahneman, *supra* at 152-54.

36. *Wikipedia: List of Cognitive Biases.*

37. Kahneman, *supra* at 293.

38. Owen D, Jones & Sarah F. Brosnan, *Law Biology, and Property: A New Theory of the Endowment Effect*, 49 Milliam & Mary L. Rev. 1935, 1942 (2008). [http://scholarship.law.wm.edu/cgi/viewcontent.cgi?article=1160&context=wmlr]

39. *Id.* at 1939.

40. *Id.* at 1945.

41. Kahneman, *supra* at 294.

42. Jones & Brosnan, *supra* at 1943.

43. Kahneman, *supra* at 296.

44. Jones & Brosnan, *supra* at 1953-63.

45. *Id.* at 1956.

46. *Id.*

47. *Id.* at 1957.

48. *Id.* at 1959.

49. *Id.* at 1960.

50. Steven Bradley, *The Framing Effect: Influence Your Audience By Setting The Context*, Vanseo Design (June 7, 2010). [http://vanseodesign.com/web-design/framing-expectation-exposure-effect/]

51. *Id.*

52. Kahneman, *supra* at 367.

53. Bradley, *supra*.

54. Irwin P. Levin et,al, *A New Look at Framing Effects: Distribution of Effect Sizes, Individual Differences, and Independence of Types of Effects*, (2002). [http://citeseerx.ist.psu.edu/viewdoc/download?doi=10.1.1.203.2745&rep=rep1&type=pdf]

55. Bradley, *supra*.

56. *Wikipedia: Framing Effect (Psychology)*. [https://en.wikipedia.org/wiki/Framing_effect_(psychology)]

57. Kahneman, *supra* at 353-62.

58. Bradley, *supra*.

59. Kahneman, *supra* at 363.

60. *Id.* at 364.

61. Michael A. Kamins & Lawrence J. Marks, *The Effect of Framing and Advertising Sequencing on Attitude Consistency and Behavioral Intentions*, 14 Advances in Consumer Research 168 (1987). [http://www.acrwebsite.org/volumes/6678/volumes/v14/NA-14]

62. Justin Zackel, *Is It Better to Interview First or Last?* [https://www.higheredjobs.com/articles/articleDisplay.cfm?ID=662]

63. *Wikipedia: Gambler's Fallacy*. [https://en.wikipedia.org/wiki/Gambler's_fallacy]

64. *Id.*

65. *Id.*

66. Kahneman, *supra* at 117.

67. *Wikipedia: Gambler's Fallacy*.

68. Jeremy Smith, *Six Advantages of Hyperbolic Discounting...And What The Heck Is It Anyway?*, [https://blog.kissmetrics.com/hyperbolic-discounting/]

69. *Wikipedia: Hyperbolic Discounting.* [https://en.wikipedia.org/wiki/Hyperbolic_discounting]

70. *Id.*

71. *Id.*

72. *Id.*

73. Smith, *supra.*

74. *Id.*

75. *Wikipedia: List of Cognitive Biases.*

76. Sara Robertson, *Loss Aversion*, Being Human (April 1, 2013). [http://www.beinghuman.org/article/loss-aversion]

77. *Wikipedia: Loss Aversion.* [https://en.wikipedia.org/wiki/Loss_aversion] Kahneman estimates it at 1.5 to 2.5. Kahneman, *supra* at 284.

78. *Id..*

79. Robertson, *supra.*

80. Kahneman, *supra* at 311-314.

81. *Id.* at 343.

82. *Id.* at 312.

83. *Id.* at 336-40.

84. *Id.* at 339.

85. *Id.* at 344-45.

86. *Id.* at 345.

87. *Wikipedia: List of Cognitive Biases.*

88. Lee Ross, *Reactive Devaluation in Negotiation and Conflict Resolution*, [http://law.stanford.edu/wp-content/uploads/sites/default/files/child-page/370999/doc/slspublic/Reactive%20Devaluation.pdf]

89. *Wikipedia: Reactive Devaluation*, Barriers to Conflict Resolution. [https://en.wikipedia.org/wiki/Reactive_devaluation]

90. *Wikipedia: List of Cognitive Biases.*

91. Robert L. Leahy, *Letting Go of Sunk Costs*, Psychology Today (Sept. 24, 2014). [https://www.psychologytoday.com/blog/anxiety-files/201409/letting-go-sunk-costs]

92. *Id.*

93. Robert Nozick, The Nature of Rationality (1993).

94. Kahneman, *supra* at 277. Theory-induced blindness is not limited to economic biases, but it is convenient to discuss it here.

95. *Id.*

96. *Id.* at 306.

97. Based on *Id.* at 307.

98. Owen D. Jones, *Why Behavioral Economics Isn't Better, and How it Could Be*, Research Handbook on Behavioral Law and Economics (J.C. Teitelbaum & K. Zeiler eds, 2015). [http://ssrn.com/abstract=2504776]

99. Kahneman, *supra* at 222-23.

100. *Id.* at 223.

101. *Id.*

102. *Id.* at 224.

103. *Id.* at 225.

104. *Id.* at 226.

105. *Id.* at 232-33.

106. *Id.* at 229.

107. *Id.* at 231-32.

108. *Id.* at 185.

109. *Id.*

110. *Id.*

111. *Id.* at 241.

112. *Id.* at 187.

113. *Id.* at 190.

114. Based on *Id.*

115. *Id.*

116. *Id.* at 191.

Chapter Six
Cognitive Biases and Practical Reasoning

Chapter Goals.
1. To discuss practical reasoning in detail.
2. To show how the use of practical reasoning can help lawyers overcome some cognitive biases.
3. To show how cognitive biases can affect practical reasoning.

    The last four chapters have introduced you to the most important cognitive biases, and they have shown how they can affect both everyday life and law practice. It is now time to discuss the cognitive biases in more complex settings. This chapter will show how practical (moral) reasoning can help an attorney overcome cognitive biases, and how cognitive biases affect practical reasoning. Practical reasoning is a System 2 tool (intentional deliberation) that helps you slow down your thinking. Legal scholars have suggested that practical reasoning can help new lawyers–and law students– "more systematically approach their ethical thinking and behavior."[1]

I. An Introduction to Practical Reasoning

    "Practical reason [or practical wisdom] is the general human capacity for resolving, through reflection, the question of what one is to do."[2] Practical wisdom is–"the right way to do the right thing in a particular circumstance, with a particular person, at a particular time"[3] or "the integration of moral will with moral skill with nuanced empathy and imagination."[4] It helps prevent thinkers from jumping to conclusions based on faulty intuitions. Moreover, it allows more nuanced decisions than decisions based solely on rules.[5] (rule-based thinking versus reflective thinking)
    Practical wisdom involves deliberately "(1) balancing competing values with empathy and detachment, (2) considering the variable courses of action and the consequences to others from each option, and (3) resolving the question in a way that is the best alternative in the circumstances."[6] [←three-part test] The ability to balance conflicting interests includes one's own good against the good of others.[7] Moreover, you need to understand that the choices are not black and white; there is usually more than one answer, and few answers are perfect.
    There are four capacities for accomplishing ethical actions based on the theory of psychologist James Rest: 1) moral sensitivity, 2) moral judgment, 3) moral motivation, and 4) moral implementation.[8] <u>Moral sensitivity</u> is the ability to recognize that a moral or ethical problem exists and the extent of that problem.[9] It also involves the available actions and the effects of each action.[10] <u>Moral judgment</u> is the ability "to reason through alternative outcomes to the correct decision."[11] In other words, "which line of action is more morally justified."[12] <u>Moral motivation</u> is the motivation to act morally.[13] It requires the ability to resist economic and cultural pressures that tend to pull people in the wrong direction. Moral motivation is mainly based on intrinsic values rather than self-interest or extrinsic rewards, such as prestige, money, praise, and publicity.[14] Scholars have shown that moral motivation depends on an individual's experiences and influences, including education.[15] Finally, <u>moral implementation</u> is "the ability and the will to carry out the moral result," and it "requires courage, resolve, and ego strength."[16] As two authors have asserted, "A person may be sensitive to moral issues,

have good judgment, and prioritize moral values; but if he or she is lacking in moral character and competence, he or she may wilt under pressure or fatigue, may not follow through, may be distracted or discouraged, and moral behavior will fail."[17]

Exercises VI-1A

1. Do you understand the three-part test for applying practical wisdom I presented above? If not reread it. [I will discuss the parts of this test in more detail below.]
2. Do you understand why I also gave you Rest's four capacities?
3. Describe Rest's four capacities in your own words.
4. Do you have a well-developed moral sensitivity? Think about times in your life when you have used or not used moral sensitivity in an important situation. Recognizing a moral problem is a major step in solving it.
5. When faced with an ethical/moral dilemma can you rationally reason through the alternatives? [This is the stage in which Rest overlaps with the three-part test.]
6. Is moral motivation easy for you? At times in your life have you lacked moral motivation? Think about people–real or fictional–who have exhibited moral motivation.
7. Do you have the courage and resolve of moral implementation? Think of times in your life when you have exhibited or lacked moral implementation. Think about people–real or fictional–who have lacked moral implementation. Why couldn't they do the right thing?
8. Think about how you can apply the process to some of the ethical dilemmas you have faced in your life. Think about how you felt when you failed morally.
9. Fiction can show you how people have exercised or failed to exercise moral judgment. Think about fictional characters who have faced moral dilemmas and how they handled them.

A. The Three-Part Test Empathy

"Empathy is the capacity to understand or feel what another person is experiencing from within the other being's frame of reference, i.e., the capacity to place oneself in another's position. Empathy is seeing with the eyes of another, listening with the ears of another and feelings with the heart of another.[18] In other words, <u>put yourself in the other person's shoes</u>.

Think up several ethical dilemmas concerning multiple parties. Try to feel empathy for all involved parties. Try to see each situation from each party's viewpoint. Don't prejudge a person's actions. Ignore their ethnicity, nationality, political affiliation, gender, education, and other irrelevant traits. Initially, treat each relevant party equally. Treat each party as if his or her claim, grievance, or idea might be valid.

B. The Three-Part Test: Detachment

Think about the detachment prong of the practical wisdom test. You should initially look at an ethical problem objectively, and one way of doing this is to brainstorm. Another way is to assume the role of a mediator. A mediator tries to help opposing parties in a dispute reach a settlement. A mediator has to be completely objective to do this, or the mediation will fail.

Is it difficult for you to look at an ethical problem objectively? Can you put aside your views, what society thinks, and what you are expected to think? Try this with a few common ethical dilemmas. Later, when evaluating alternatives, you can bring in your values, the customs of your profession, and society's morality.

C. The Three-Part Test: Alternative Solutions

A key part of practical wisdom is coming up with alternative solutions. Consider all reasonable alternatives in detail. Your problem-solving (practical wisdom) will be incomplete if you do not consider all reasonable alternatives. (I've emphasized this throughout this book.) Lazy thinkers choose the first alternative; engaged thinkers consider the problem from all angles.

When choosing the best solution, consider all factors behind the alternatives. Consider the context (custom, community morality, your personal morality, practicality). Try to avoid letting your emotions get in way of making the right decisions. Weigh all alternatives carefully.

Exercise VI-1B: Evaluating and Choosing Alternatives

For the exercises below, decide which rule, policy, or practice is better. There are no right answers. Make sure that you consider all the reasons for making your choice before you select it. Then, state your reason(s) for making the choice: fairness, policy, morality, cultural practices or custom, efficiency, etc. Think about how your System 1 influenced your initial thoughts and how using your System 2 affected your decision.

1. A. A state requires that all employers carry worker's compensation insurance so that their employees will be covered in the case of injury on the job.
B. A jurisdiction does not require that their employers carry worker's compensation insurance. In this jurisdiction, employees cannot recover from their employer for on-the-job injuries unless their employers are negligent. Employees in this jurisdiction make 25% more than employees in the first jurisdiction.
2. A. A state requires that all employers carry worker's compensation insurance so that their employees will be covered in the case of injury on the job. Under worker's comp, an employee can't recover for pain and suffering from their employer.
B. This state does not have worker's compensation insurance. Employees can recover from their employers under the usual negligence rules, and they can recover for pain and suffering.
3. A. State A requires all doctors to buy malpractice insurance.
B. State B does not require that doctors buy malpractice insurance.
4. A. Country A has outlawed female circumcision by statute.
B. Country B has not.
5. A. Jurisdiction A places the burden of proof for a consent defense in a rape case on the plaintiff.

B. Jurisdiction B places the burden of proof for a consent defense in a rape case on the defendant.
6. Reconsider problem 5 with this new fact: both the plaintiff and defendant are men. (If you changed your answer, did you use System 1 or 2?)
7. A. Jurisdiction A sets the minimum drinking age at 21.
B. Jurisdiction B sets the minimum drinking age at 18.
8. A. State A forbids smoking in bars and restaurants.
B. State B does not.
9. A. The Hysteria Law Review rules require that at least 20% of its members must be ethic minorities.
B. The Eastern Hysteria Law Review does not have such a rule.
10. A. Jurisdiction A has a rule protecting unicorns, including a statute forbidding anyone from hunting them
B. A prosecutor refuses to prosecute a man under the above law because there is a severe famine in the country, and the man killed the unicorn to feed his family.
11. A. Jurisdiction A has extensive statutes protecting tenants in residential rental buildings. Jurisdiction B does not have such statutes. Apartments are 25% cheaper in jurisdiction B.
12. A. Jurisdiction A forbids the use of birth control because they want their citizens to have more babies.
B. Jurisdiction B does not have such a rule.
13. A. Jurisdiction A allows only individuals who have a law license to practice in that state.
B. Jurisdiction B allows anyone who has a college degree to practice law in simple cases such as uncontested divorces, writing wills, or writing simple contracts.
14. A. Jurisdiction A suspends a driver's license for 90 days after a drunk driving conviction.
B. Jurisdiction B suspends a driver's license for 90 days after two drunk driving convictions.
15. A. Because of overpopulation and famine, jurisdiction A limits their citizens to one child per couple.
B. Because of overpopulation and famine, jurisdiction B limits their citizens to two children per family.
C. Despite similar overpopulation and famine, jurisdiction C does not limit how many children its citizens may have.
16. A. School A has a fall fair for students during class time. The cost is $10 per student. Any students who can't pay or doesn't want to go can spend that afternoon in the library.
B. School B has a fall fair for students during class time. The cost is $20 per student. Those who can't pay can go anyway.
17. A. State A has public funding for the arts.
B. Jurisdiction B does not.
18. A. Jurisdiction A funds legal representation for indigents with a 0.25% sales tax.
B. Jurisdiction B requires that attorneys pay $500 per year to fund legal representation for indigents.
C. Jurisdiction C requires that attorneys perform fifty hours of pro bono a year.
D. Jurisdiction D does not require that attorneys perform pro bono, and it does not fund legal representation for indigents.
19. Stop and frisk is a practice where police officers stop and question a pedestrian, then frisk

them for weapons and contraband.
A. Jurisdiction A uses stop and frisk.
B. Jurisdiction B does not. The crime rate is lower in jurisdiction B.
20. A. A company pays all its employees the same regardless of their job, work quality, or experience.
B. B. A company pays its employees based on seniority.
C. A company pays its employees based on the type of job and evaluations.

D. The Four Capacities: Moral Sensitivity

Above, I mentioned James Rest's four capacities for ethical action: 1) moral sensitivity (or moral awareness), 2) moral reasoning (or judgment), 3) moral motivation, and 4) moral implementation (or moral courage). In this subsection, I will focus on moral sensitivity.

Moral sensitivity is the ability to recognize that a moral or ethical problem exists and the extent of that problem. It also involves the available actions and the effects of each action.

Most humans are born with an inner moral sensitivity. However, as I am sure you have noticed, some humans are more sensitive than others. Like many other things, such as walking, playing the piano, and learning chess, moral sensitivity needs to be developed; it needs to be practiced in the right way.

You can develop your moral sensitivity. First, you need to pay attention to the world around you. Do you watch what other people do, or do you walk around with your head down, focusing on yourself? In other words, a large part of moral sensitivity is attitude. Attitude: I will pay attention to what is happening around me. Second, you need to be aware of what others are thinking and feeling. This skill will take a long time to develop, but you can develop it if you work on it everyday. Attitude: I will pay attention to what others are thinking and feeling. Habits: I will pay attention to the waitress when she serves me lunch; I will try to discern how she is feeling. I will pay attention to how my spouse is feeling. I will try to put my self in her shoes. When I see someone acting badly, I will not immediately criticize them, but I will try to discern whether there is a reason for their bad behavior. Third, you need to be aware of the ethical implications in your actions. Attitude: when I make a decision or take an action, I will consider how it affects others. Habit: when I make a decision for my family, I will think about how it affects my spouse and children, instead of just focusing on my interest. Develop moral imagination. Think about moral dilemmas and how your actions action will affect others. Fourth, reflection helps you develop moral sensitivity. Fifth, emotion can be a part of moral sensitivity. When you react to something emotionally, think about why you are feeling this way.

Exercises VI-1C: Moral Sensitivity

1. You are seated on a crowded subway or bus. Do you notice that a standee needs to sit down because of age or health?
2. Do you notice when a friend is upset? Can you tell how upset that friend is?
3. Do you notice when a fellow employee is upset?
4. Do you notice when your boss is upset?

5. Do you think about why your children are crying?
6. Do you notice when someone is ill?
7. When you see an injustice, do you react emotionally?
8. Do you notice others who are morally sensitive?
9. Do you admire others for being morally sensitive?
10. Are your role models morally sensitive?
11. Are these ethical dilemmas or something else?

A. You see a friend shoplift. B. A friend has a drinking problem. C. You can't decide which blouse to buy. D. You only have one tv, and you and your spouse can't agree on which television program to watch. E. A city must decide whether to improve the bus system or build more highways. F. Your best friend is cheating on her spouse. G. Whether to declare all your tips on your taxes. H. You are in charge of hiring a new associate for your law firm. The best candidate is Asian. The second best candidate is African-American. I. You and a friend disagree where to eat dinner. J. Whether your company will acquire another company. K. Whether your company will conduct layoffs. L. How your company will conduct layoffs. M. You are at a restaurant, and a small child is disturbing everyone's dinner. N. You are late for work. Just as you are leaving the house, a friend calls you with a serious problem. a. You do not have a cell phone. b. You can talk to your friend on your cellphone while driving. O. You have been asked to torture a prisoner in order to get information to prevent a terrorist attack. P. A waiter shortchanges you. Q. What kind of punishment a child will receive for misbehaving. R. What kind of punishment a criminal will receive for theft. S. Your boss has told you to pad a bill.

12. Do you think the commandants of Nazi concentration camps had moral sensitivity?
13. Think of several situations in your life where you exercised moral sensitivity? Think of several situations in your life where you failed to exercise moral sensitivity?
14. How is empathy involved in moral sensitivity?
15. Two children are getting ready to throw water balloons on to the cars below on a highway. What are the possible consequences of the children's actions? If you witness this, what are your available actions?
16. A medical researcher is studying a new cancer drug. She ignores a few anomalies in the tests. What are the possible consequences?
17. Do you think about the consequences of your actions?
18. When you face an ethical dilemmas do you try to think through all possible solutions, or do you take the first alternative?
19. When you watch a movie or television or read a fictional book, try to spot the ethical dilemmas. What were the characters' available actions? What were the consequences of the characters' moral choices?

E. The Four Capacities: Moral Implementation

The other of Rest's four capacities I want to discuss in more detail is moral implementation or moral courage. This is the hardest part of practical wisdom to perform. It is one thing to be able to recognize a moral problem and choose between the alternatives, but implementing moral choices often requires an inner fortitude that many people do not have.

Here is an excellent example of moral implementation.[19] In 2002, Cynthia Cooper, vice-president of internal audit, and her colleagues discovered massive fraud (inflating profits) at WorldCom, a major telecommunications company. She disclosed the fraud to the auditing committee of WorldCom's board.
Professor Timothy Floyd wrote about Cooper:

> Cooper is an outstanding moral example for law students and lawyers. Cooper was faced with an enormous challenge at WorldCom. . . . She is a hero because she did the right thing in the face of overwhelming pressures to keep silent. The characteristics we admire in her were moral vision and moral courage–the vision to see what was really going on, despite the pressures to look the other way, and the courage to act on what she knew was right, despite harmful consequences to herself.[20]

There are a mountain of examples of those who have exercised moral courage. When I was growing up one of my favorite books was John F. Kennedy's *Profiles in Courage*. It describes the moral courage of eight U.S. Senators at great cost to themselves. Think of some examples where individuals have exercised moral courage.

Of course, there are numerous examples in which individuals did not exercise moral courage. You can start with the many employees at WorldCom who failed to disclose its fraud before Cooper and her team did. You can think of the many people who failed to stand up to southern segregationists in the 50s and 60s. Obviously, there are those who failed to halt the Holocaust during World War II. Think of other examples where individuals failed to exercise moral courage.

Of course, moral courage doesn't just happen on the world stage; it occurs in everyday life. In one of my classes, two students turned in another student for cheating. That took moral courage. Someone who testifies at a criminal trial has moral courage. In fact, it requires moral courage when anyone speaks up against any wrong.

Think of times in your life when you have exercised moral courage and times in your life when you have not.

At this point, I was going to ask you whether you thought you could exercise moral courage like Cynthia Cooper did. However, this would be a very unfair question. No one knows how they are going to act until they face the difficult situation. Still, you should think about your future actions and be prepared when a difficult situation arises. I guarantee that they will occur.

Summation: Applying Practical Wisdom.

1. Try to view ethical problems (initially) with detachment. (A way to develop detachment is to brainstorm. Write down all the possible alternatives without being critical. Later, you can criticize the alternatives.)
2. Try to feel empathy for all persons involved in a situation. Ask yourself, how would I feel if I were in that person's shoes?
3. Fully consider all alternative courses of action and all the consequences of those actions. Try to discern indirect consequences (what might be unforeseen consequences to others).

4. Develop your ability to select the best alternative through moral judgment. This often involves weighing interests.

II. Cognitive Biases and Practical Reasoning in the Law

Using practical reasoning can help you avoid cognitive biases in your thought processes because it slows down your thinking and it requires you to reason step-by-step. Think of several instances in your law practice where practical reasoning could have helped you make a decision.

Practical reasoning, however, is also subject to the influence of cognitive biases. Below, I will show how cognitive biases can affect the four steps of Rest's method.

Many cognitive biases can cause us to miss moral dilemmas. A major impediment to moral sensitivity is framing. The way a question is framed can cause someone to not see the ethical problem. Similarly, emotional factors, such as guilt, shame, low self-esteem, and seeking the approval pf others, can cause an individual to be blind to ethical lapses.[21] Likewise, the overconfidence bias can make us think that we are good at avoiding ethical problems. The Semmelweis reflex can then make us ignore the overconfidence effect when we fail to allow new evidence to overcome our view that we are ethical. Finally, other factors, such as focusing on another problem, focusing on the technical aspects of a project, identification with a role (management versus technical), time pressures, and fatigue can impede moral awareness.[22]

Cognitive biases can also interfere with moral reasoning–what "ought" to be done. This step involves coming up with the right moral answer, and anything that affects this process, such as overreliance on System 1, can result in the wrong normative conclusion. Obviously, the empathy gap can interfere with moral reasoning. Understanding the feelings of oneself and others is vital in determining what the proper moral decision is. Likewise, a confirmation bias can interfere with moral reasoning because it can make a person too confident in the validity of her answer. Any bias that interferes with the full gathering and consideration of all relevant information, such as the expectation bias, Semmelweis reflex and in-group bias, can also cause problems.

Concerning moral motivation, scholars distinguish between two selves: 1) the "should" self, which "is motivated to act on the conclusion of our moral" reasoning and 2) the "want" self, which "is motivated to act on what's in our best interest."[23] The want self may be motivated by professional gain, the desire to avoid criticism, and conformity with others.[24] Can you see the possible cognitive biases in these, especially the negativity biases?

Moral implementation involves the individual having the moral courage to carry out the decision. "Moral agents must overcome active opposition, cope with fatigue, resist distractions, and develop sophisticated strategies for reaching their goals. In sum, they must persist in a moral task or action despite obstacles."[25] Negativity biases especially affect this stage for lawyers. "What if" I reported the senior partner for unethical conduct. I'd never get another good assignment. I would probably be fired at the next associate evaluation. I couldn't get a good reference from this firm, so I probably would never have a good legal job again.

Problems

Cognitive Biases and Practical Reasoning

Think through the four steps in Rest's approach with the following problems. Consider how cognitive biases are involved.

1. You are inside counsel for a car company. The company has discovered that its newest model has a significant (and deadly) problem with brake failure. The CEO believes that the cost of lawsuits would be less than the cost of fixing the problem. Reason through your moral dilemma.
2. Your elderly client, who probably has dementia, has asked you to write his will. He has three grandchild. He suggests that you should be the primary beneficiary of his vast estate. What do you do?
3. You've screwed up big this time, and you cost your client the case. However, you have an out. Another associate working on the case has just quit the firm and moved to remote Alaska to be a missionary. What do you do?
4. You are a prosecutor on the case of a serial rapist, who has escaped punishment for several crimes. A witness comes to you and says that he was with the rapist at the time of his latest crime. He sat near him in a bar on the night of the attack. You think the witness is being truthful, but that he might be mistaken about the identification. You don't want the rapist to be found not guilty again this time because you know he will continue to be a predator. Do you notify the defendant's attorney about the possible alibi witness?

Notes

1. Milton C. Regan, Jr. & Nancy L. Sachs, *Ain't Misbehaving": Ethical Pitfalls and Rest's Model of Moral Judgment,"* 51 N.E. L, Rev. 53, 32 (2017).

2. *Stanford Encyclopedia of Philosophy: Practical Reason.* [http://plato.stanford.edu/entries/practical-reason/]

3. Barry Schwartz & Kenneth Sharpe, *Practical Wisdom: The Right Way to Do the Right Thing*, 85 (2010).

4. Roberto L. Corrada & David Thomson, *Report on the 2012 Conference and Introduction to the 2013 Conference: The Development of Professional Identity in Legal Education: Rethinking Learning and Assessment*, at *9 (Educating Tomorrow's Lawyers 2013).

5. Daisy Hurst Floyd, *Practical Wisdom: Reimagining Legal Education*, 10 U. St. Thomas L.J. 195, 205 (2013) ("When conduct is guided only by rules, judgment is distorted.").

6. Benjamin V. Madison III, *The Emperor has No Clothes but Does Anyone Really Care? How Law Schools are Failing to Develop Students' Professional Identities and Practical Reasoning*, http://papers.ssrn.com/sol3/papers.cfm?abstract_id=2414015, at *43 (2014)

7. *Id.* at *10. Professor Madison elaborated: "Reaching a judgment requires not only self-knowledge so as to avoid having one's own motives interfere in the decision-making. In the real world where questions and answers fall into a gray area, one must consider all of the possible courses of actions, who will be affected and how, and do so with the specifics of the context in mind. Such decisions will necessarily recognize that a judgment, while favoring one or more values, will simultaneously decide against one or more other competing values." *Id.* at *18.

8. Floyd, *supra* at 208-211; *see also* Neil W. Hamilton & Verna Monson, *Legal Education's Ethical Challenge: Empirical Research on How Most Effectively to Foster Each Students Professional Formation (Professionalism)*, 9 St. Thomas L. Rev. 325, 346-49 (2011); James R. Rest, Background Theory and Research *in* Moral Development of the Professions: Psychology and Applied Ethics 1, 22–25 (James R. Rest & Darcia Narvaez eds., 1994).

9. Floyd, *supra* at 208.

10. Muriel J. Bebeau & Verna E. Monson, *Guided by Theory, Grounded in Evidence: A Way Forward for Professional Ethics Education*, *in* HANDBOOK OF MORAL AND CHARACTER EDUCATION 558 (Larry P. Nucci & Darcia Narvaez eds, 2008).

11. Floyd, *supra* at 208.

12. Bebeau & Monson, *supra* at 558.

13. Floyd, *supra* at 209-210.

14. *Id.* Two authors have added, "Whether the individual gives priority to moral concerns seems to be a function of how deeply moral notions penetrate self-understanding, that is, whether moral considerations are judged constitutive of the self. For behavior to occur, the moral agents must first decide on a morally correct action when faced with a dilemma, and then conclude that the self is responsible for that action. One is motivated to perform an action just because the self is at stake and on the line—just because the self is responsible. Moral motivation is a function of an internal drive for self-consistency." Bebeau & Monson, *supra* at 558.

15. Floyd, *supra* at 209-210. Ironically, research has demonstrated that lawyers are happier if they are motivated by intrinsic factors rather than extrinsic ones. *Id.*

16. *Id.* at 210.

17. Bebeau & Monson, *supra* at 558.

18. *Wikipedia: Empathy* [https://en.wikipedia.org/wiki/Empathy]

19. Timothy W. Floyd, *Moral Vision, Moral Courage, and the Formation of a Lawyer's Professional Identity*, http://www.teachinglegalethics.org/sites/default/files/TimFloydMoralVisionMoralCourageFormationOfLawyersProfessionalIdentity-28MissCLR339-2009.pdf.

20. *Id.* at 339-40.

21. Regan & Sachs, *supra* at 59.

22. Id. at 60-65.

23. *Id,* at 69.

24. *Id.* at 70.

25. Craig E. Johnson, Organizational Ethics: A Practical Approach 71 (2011).

Chapter Seven
Behavioral Legal Ethics

I. Behavioral Legal Ethics

In recent years, a new field has emerged within ethics–behavioral ethics, which modifies traditional thinking on ethics.[1] Much of traditional ethics was based on the notion that human beings are rational thinkers–that they act in their best interests. Behavioral ethics has rejected this view based on the research discussed throughout this book. Rather, behavioral ethicists believe in "bounded rationality" in which rational thinking is affected by defects in the human thinking process.[2] Furthermore "Behavioral ethicists describe the actual behavior of people, how situational and social forces influence it, and they study ways in which decisions can be nudged in a more ethical direction through simple interventions."[3] As we have discussed before, the defects in the thinking process occurred because of evolution; these defects are remnants of mankind's survival mechanisms and need to propagate his or her genes.

It should be no surprise that some legal ethicists have adopted the insights of behavioral ethics, with a field of behavioral legal ethics emerging in the last ten years.[4] The idea behind this approach is that not only should legal ethics study the rules and punishments of legal ethics using a normative approach,[5] but that the how and why of legal ethics should also be studied. In other words, ethicists should study human behavior in addition to the normative aspects of legal ethics.

Behavioral legal ethics is a descriptive approach, and it "focuses on two elements: an individual's actual behavior and the psychological processes that underlie that behavior."[6] One scholar has observed, "this objective analysis would likely uncover a 'gap' between the attorney's beliefs about his behavior and his actual behavior—between what, if given the opportunity, he would predict he would do under any given circumstance, and what he actually does when confronted with the ethical decision."[7] Stated differently, "the central idea is that unethical conduct is frequently the product of psychological factors that occur largely outside of the conscious awareness of the decision-maker. The result is that well-intentioned lawyers will often be unaware of how their behavior diverges from their own conceptions of themselves as ethical and honest people."[8] A good example of this new approach is the analysis of David Boies's unethical conduct that began this book. As you may remember, Mr. Boies represented Harvey Weinstein in his sexual harassment problems, as well as the New York Times, which had an interest in revealing Mr. Weinstein's misdeeds. Although a neutral observer would call this a flagrant ethical breach, Mr. Weinstein did not see it this way. He mistakenly thought that he could avoid this conflict because of ethical (or moral) blindness and the overconfidence effect.

The most important type of cognitive bias for legal ethics is ethical (or moral) blindness–unintentional unethical conduct.[9] Under this cognitive bias, an individual fails to see that there is an ethical problem (ethical fading). Thus, an ethical lapse may be unintentional, in contrast to traditional ethics analysis that views all ethical lapses as intentional.[10] An ethical violator may not be a bad person; "a conscientious attorney can unintentionally make a poor ethical decision."[11] As we saw in the previous chapter, ethical awareness requires moral sensitivity. For example, a person may think that lying to the court is repugnant, but he does so himself because he doesn't realize he is lying or can rationalize his lying. (As I mentioned in Chapter One, when you find yourself rationalizing, it is a big hint that you are suffering from a cognitive bias.) Similarly, under ethical fading, "ethical dimen-sions are eliminated or faded from a problem to be solved because other aspects of the decision, such as business, strategic, or client's best interest considerations dominate the framing process."[12] In other words, framing can cause someone to not see an ethical dilemma. Finally, relying too much on System 1 or not getting enough information (anchoring, availability heuristic, etc.) can produce ethical blindness.

One of the causes of ethical blindness is faulty emotional prediction.[13] In making predictions about the future, most people believe that they can act objectively. This is wrong; in any future situation, emotions will affect how the individual behaves, and, consequently, will affect her ethics.

Related to the above is situational ethics: People will act differently based on the context. In other words, there is a disconnect between one's moral code, and how one acts in a particular situation.[14] This is because morality is malleable and dynamic, rather than fixed.[15] In addition, individuals often emphasis the "pragmatic self" over the "idealistic self."[16] For example, a young associate might make an ethical mistake when working for a firm that has lax ethics. This is because people tend to behave like their in-group–in this case, their law firm.[17] Other situational factors include "age, nationality, psychological state, working conditions and observed behavior of others."[18] Finally, just being in a partisan role, as is the case in litigation, can affect a lawyer's ethics (the "partisanship problem").[19]

A bias I discussed earlier–the bias blind spot–also affects ethical blindness. "When people disagree, they often ascribe a bias to each other, while believing themselves to be objective."[20]

Another problem that may cause ethical blindness is the "slippery slope" or ethical numbness."[21] This begins with minor infractions that lead to more serious ones. For example, an attorney may initially ignore a minor conflict of interest. Next, he ignores more serious ones. Finally, he commits serious breaches of conflict of interest. One scholar has described this process as "Efforts to reduce cognitive dissonance—the uncomfortable feeling experienced when actions are inconsistent with beliefs—can result in a new lawyer incrementally changing his ethical standards to match actual ethical decisions and behavior."[22] The slippery slope occurs because morality is malleable and dynamic.

Finally, a person may have a script for how to handle situations that might involve ethics, such as conflicts of interest.[23] When something is not on that script, the lawyer doesn't recognize the problem as a possible conflict, and a violation may occur. For example, an attorney once explained, "when you're dealing with big companies, it [ethical issues] doesn't seem to come up."[24] Other examples include routine services, such as "maintaining sufficient support staff, or communicating with clients."[25]

Compounding the problem of ethical blindness is that the human brain is poor at recognizing its mistakes.[26] People "dread" realizing they have made a mistake so the unconscious often covers up mistakes through "motivated reasoning"—"the empirically demonstrated tendency for people to reach the conclusion they prefer, especially if they have a vested personal interest in the result."[27] Moreover, "overconfidence in their original predictions shielded them from recognizing, in hindsight, that their predictions were mistaken" (poor self-assessment).[28] Other cognitive processes that affect a person's inability to see her mistakes include the confirmation bias, cognitive dissonance, and situational effects.[29] Even if a person recognizes his mistake, cognitive biases will make it difficult for him to acknowledge it.[30]

Another major cause of ethical violations for lawyers is the overconfidence effect, which I discussed in detail in Chapter Two. With the overconfidence effect, a lawyer recognizes a possible ethical problem but believes she can avoid it, even though she realizes that most lawyers can't. For example, I think Mr. Boies was suffering from the overconfidence effect in connection with his simultaneously handling of Harvey Weinstein and the New York Times. Similarly, an attorney may believe that he can have an affair with a client without any problems, although he knows of similar situations that resulted in complaints to the state bar.

Many other cognitive biases can affect an attorney's ethics. Here are a few:

Framing can affect how a lawyer views an ethical dilemma. In the last chapter, I discussed how framing might cause an attorney not to see the ethical issue at all. Framing can also affect other aspects of a case. For example, people "are more likely to behave unethically to avoid losses than to obtain gains."[31] Similarly, how you frame a settlement could affect whether the otherside accepts it.

Euphemisms can cause one to downplay the ethical implications of an act.[32] For example, Republicans accused Attorney General Loretta Lynch of unethical conduct when she changed "investigation" into "matter" during the investigation of Hillary Clinton's emails.

People are less likely to see an ethical problem when it doesn't result in harm (outcome bias).[33] For example, a lawyer may see no ethical problem with a clear conflict of interest that caused no harm. However, if the bar only punished unethical conduct when it caused harm, might this cause even more unethical conduct because of the cognitive biases discussed above?

People are more likely to ignore unethical behavior when it takes place through an intermediary.[34] (This is one reason people hire lawyers.) "Because harms caused indirectly entail less moral intensity than harms inflicted directly, people tend to be more willing to engage in unethical conduct when acting through an agent than when acting for themselves."[35]

Economic factors can obviously influence how a lawyer views an ethical decision. A lawyer needs to be able to earn a living. However, other interests, such as the client's interests or the public's interest, may conflict with this. Problems arise when this happens because the attorney cannot be "objective" about his own economic interests.

Group dynamics can affect cognitive processing. "People may do bad things as part of a group, even though they may never consider doing so when acting alone."[36] On the other hand, people can change strongly held beliefs when influenced by their social groups.[37]

Cognitive framing by a group of attorneys' shared understanding of a problem can shape how an individual sees that problem, even though a person might see the problem differently if she were working on the problem on her own.[38]

Finally, as stated earlier, emotions often affect ethics by producing faulty reasoning. Among the emotions that help people act ethically are the inner-directed emotions of guilt (which they tend to feel when they act immorally) and shame (which they tend to feel when others discover that they have acted immorally). Outer-directed emotions include anger and disgust, which people tend to feel toward others who violate accepted moral standards."[39]

Understanding and Overcoming Cognitive Biases for Lawyers and Law Students

Now, see how you do with the following exercises on behavioral legal ethics.

Cognitive Biases Exercises

Identify the possible cognitive biases.

1. Why would a prosecutor continue to prosecute someone when DNA evidence shows that the defendant is not guilty?
2. An attorney "borrows" a client's settlement fund for a couple of weeks because she is short of cash.
3. It's right on the line, but I can represent both these clients.
4. This conduct is ethical. Everyone in my firm does it.
5. Should I give this big case to another attorney because I've never done a case like this before? No, I'm fine.
6. I know that this attorney has had ethical problems in the past, but I'm going to hire her anyway. I can make sure she does nothing wrong.
7. The client will want to take the settlement. I would if I were him.
8. I am advising my client to continue the case. I know we only have a small chance of winning, but she has already spent over a million dollars in attorney's fees.
9. I know that the client wants to accept the settlement, but I am advising against it. I have litigated several cases against the other attorney, and I'm sure she is doing something dishonest.
10. I am advising my client to settle the case. I just can't deal with it anymore.

Answers

1. Anchoring, confirmation bias, expectation bias, Semmelweis reflex.
2. Overconfidence effect (I will be able to repay the money), ethical blind spot (I am only borrowing the money), framing effect, emotional reasoning.
3. Ethical blind spot, overconfidence effect.
4. Bandwagon effect, halo effect.
5. Endowment effect, optimism biases.
6. Ostrich effect, illusion of control.
7. Projection bias.
8. Sunken cost fallacy.
9. Reactive devaluation.
10. Emotional reasoning.

Reflection Exercises

1. Reflect on how the context might affect the ethics of employing different kinds of attorney's fees. Write out a list. Are the potential cognitive biases different for the type of attorney's fee?
2. Reflect on why an attorney in a public defender's office might not be a zealous advocate for all her clients?

Behavioral Legal Ethics

3. Do you think attorneys at large firms or small firms are more ethical?
4. Consider whether a judge should decide her own recusal.
5. Think about times when the "illusion of objectivity" affected your work.
6. Think of several instance where a "slippery slope" can grow from a minor offense into a major ethical breach.
7. Because the ethical rules generally provide the minimum for attorney conduct, might this cause more ethical violations because of moral blindness and the slippery slope?
8. In litigation, a lawyer's job is often to argue that a client's conduct was proper. In other words, the lawyer is offering a justification (rationalization?) after the fact. Reflect on how cognitive biases affect this process.
9. Doesn't the above apply generally to our adversarial system? In other words, don't cognitive biases cause significant ethical problems for lawyer due to the basis of our legal system?
10. Lawyers and clients often have conflicting interests. For example, a client may want to win a case at all costs, while the lawyer wants to avoid being disbarred. Reflect on how cognitive biases affect this type of situation.
11. Reflect on how cognitive biases affect negotiations.
12. If you knew that most attorneys in your jurisdiction violated an ethical rule, would you feel free to violate it, too?
13. Is it easier or harder to see unethical conduct in a friend than in an opposing attorney?
14. Think about the consequences of a hiding a mistake from a client. For example, an attorney once made up a settlement agreement to hide that he had missed a statute of limitations deadline. His fraud was later discovered. What do you think happened to him?
15. Think how framing has caused you not to see an ethical problem.
16. Do you think that inside lawyers or outside counsel are better at determining whether a company's officers are acting ethically?
17. This book argues that many ethical violations are caused by unconscious factors. How do you think this should affect sanctions for ethical violations? How should this affect law student and attorney training?
18. A client comes to you with a consumer fraud lawsuit. You think it will be a great class action. The client doesn't want to pursue it as a class action. What do you do? How might cognitive biases be involved?
19. Reread the framing section in Chapter Five. Think of ten ways framing might affect a lawyer. In litigation, in negotiations, when dealing with a client, when dealing with a judge, etc.
20. How far can attorney go in preparing a witness. Might the attorney's use of cognitive biases affect the witnesses testimony? How well can the attorney tell if this is happening? In a criminal case, might the police or prosecution's questioning of the witness affect the witness's understanding of what he observed? How can you counter this?

Comments

3. Did you answer the type of firm you work at? Was your answer influenced by a cognitive bias?

Understanding and Overcoming Cognitive Biases for Lawyers and Law Students

7. This is why I advocate that all law schools include professional identity training.

Problems

1. You suspect that your client is going to lie on the stand in a civil case. What do you do? How might cognitive biases affect your thinking? Does it make a difference if your client is a criminal defendant?

Here is the ABA Model Rule:

(a) A lawyer shall not knowingly:

   (3) offer evidence that the lawyer knows to be false. If a lawyer, the lawyer's client, or a witness called by the lawyer, has offered material evidence and the lawyer comes to know of its falsity, the lawyer shall take reasonable remedial measures, including, if necessary, disclosure to the tribunal. A lawyer may refuse to offer evidence, other than the testimony of a defendant in a criminal matter, that the lawyer reasonably believes is false.

(b) A lawyer who represents a client in an adjudicative proceeding and who knows that a person intends to engage, is engaging or has engaged in criminal or fraudulent conduct related to the proceeding shall take reasonable remedial measures, including, if necessary, disclosure to the tribunal.

Do you think that lawyers interpret this rule broadly or narrowly? Why? Might cognitive biases be involved? What is the key word in the rule that might be affected by a lawyer's cognitive biases? Is a broad or narrow interpretation best for the interests of justice?

2. You find a document while preparing a discovery response that would destroy your client's case. The document is clearly covered by a request for production of documents? What do you do? Consider how cognitive biases might be involved.

3. You hear that an unnamed attorney has been accused of stealing client funds. You consider this to be terrible. A few days later, you discover that the attorney was your best friend. Does this change your view of the occurrence?

4. Model Rule 5.2 states "(b) A subordinate lawyer does not violate the Rules of Professional Conduct if that lawyer acts in accordance with a supervisory lawyer's reasonable resolution of an arguable question of professional duty." What factors should a subordinate attorney consider when evaluating a problem under this rule? Start first with a traditional analysis, then consider cognitive biases.

5. A former client comes to you with a big case that is not in your usual area of practice. You take the case despite this fact. What rule is involved? What are the cognitive biases?

6. Write down the five most important ways prosecutors might be involved in unethical conduct. How might cognitive biases affect these?

7. How might scripts affect a debt collection practice?

8. How might cognitive biases affect an attorney's duty of zealous representation with his duty of openness to the court?

9. A basketball program has been accused of NCAA violations. Would it be better to investigate the violations with university lawyers or an outside law firm?

10. Why might adequate disclosure not be enough to avoid conflicts of interest?

11. When I was teaching a class in legal ethics, a student asked what an attorney should do when they know the opposing attorney is acting unethically, but the attorney can't prove it.

Should the first attorney act unethically, too? What would you have told the student?

12. Why do many attorneys honestly argue that they have done nothing wrong when they have been accused of ethical misconduct?

13. May a lawyer ethically represent both a passenger and a driver in a personal injury case arising from an automobile collision with another vehicle? What cognitive biases might be involved here?

14. You are a lawyer for the defense department. You have been asked whether a certain type of "torture," which the DOD wants to start using, is legal under U.S. and international law. What cognitive biases might affect your decision?

15. Model Rule 1.15 states: "a) A lawyer shall hold property of clients or third persons that is in a lawyer's possession in connection with a representation separate from the lawyer's own property. Funds shall be kept in a separate account maintained in the state where the lawyer's office is situated, or elsewhere with the consent of the client or third person." Why did the ABA enact this rule?

Comment

1. This problem is an example of a situation in which the client's interests and the interests of justice collide. Because of cognitive biases, the attorney will try to interpret the rule narrowly with the key word being "know." Do you think that lawyers usually can take an objective view of what it means to "know" when interpreting this rule? Can you? Does it help if you also consider the interests of justice when interpreting the rule?

I was once involved in a trial where the otherside put on a witness to rebut key evidence favoring our client. The witness was visibly nervous and sweat was pouring off of him. Which side do you think won the case? Did the opposing attorney help his client by putting on the witness? Can you see how cognitive biases might have been involved?

Here is another example. Model Rule 3.3 states:

(a) A lawyer shall not knowingly:

(2) fail to disclose to the tribunal legal authority in the controlling jurisdiction known to the lawyer to be directly adverse to the position of the client and not disclosed by opposing counsel.

The interpretation of this rule initially lies with the attorney. Most attorney's think that they can objectively interpret the rule, but they might be suffering from an ethical blind spot and the overconfidence effect. Under the ethical blind spot, a lawyer won't realize that his System 1 is telling him to favor his client. Similarly, with the overconfidence effect, the attorney may believe she can act objectively when others can't. However, it is hard to be objective when that objectivity will hurt the client.

What the attorney needs to do is to look at the purpose behind the rule–that cases are to be decided on the law, not mistakes made by one of the attorneys. The attorney should also try to look at the situation from the judge's viewpoint. In the end, the attorney may have to consult with another attorney in her firm that is not involved in the case. In doing so, the attorney should not tell the other attorney which side would be favored by having the case before the court. Just ask the attorney "do you think this case is on point in relation to the facts?"

Regardless of the ethics involved in the case, it is always best to disclose controlling adverse authority because this gives you the opportunity to distinguish it. The judge will probably find it any way, and, if he does, you will be in a lot of trouble. So, I hope you can see that allowing your biases to cause you to break a rule can have bad practical consequences for you and your client.

2. The only answer under traditional ethical training is to produce the document. Yet there are many cases where attorneys violated this rule. Are they bad people, or are their cognitive biases in play? Of course, the answer is sometimes one, sometimes the other. A dishonest attorney would just not produce the document, and probably wouldn't try to rationalize the decision. But consider how cognitive biases might be involved. I said the document was clearly covered by the discovery request. However, your cognitive biases might cause the attorney to question this. The attorney might also be convinced that his client should win the case based on an earlier evaluation of the case. She may then concluded that the document is not important (Semmelweis effect) so she doesn't produce it. Biases can get an attorney into a lot of trouble. If the document turns up later, a bar complaint will probably be filed against the attorney.

3. This hypo is based on the Penn State child molestation case. In this case, an assistant coach at Penn State had been accused of molesting young boys. Yet no one at Penn State did anything. Why?

I think the halo effect was involved here. The coach was a friend and colleague, so others had problems viewing him as a bad man. Other biases that might be involved concern a variation on the bandwagon effect, empathy gap, emotional reasoning, dichotomous thinking, and the ostrich effect.

4. This is a difficult problem for a young attorney, but one he must make frequently if he is going to be an ethical attorney. The first thing the attorney will probably think about is what happens to me if I report my boss? What effect will this have on my career? This is natural, but it shows the types of problems that rise in typical ethical analysis.

The key words here are "reasonable resolution of an arguable question of professional duty." This is a situation that is subject to ethical blindness. A traditional approach would assume that an attorney can make an objective evaluation of this phrase. However, the practical pressures make deciding against the boss very difficult. A solution would be for a law firm to have a senior attorney that young associations could go to anonymously and without fear of retribution.

5. Rule 1.1 Competence

A lawyer shall provide competent representation to a client. Competent representation requires the legal knowledge, skill, thoroughness and preparation reasonably necessary for the representation.

Ethical blindness, overconfidence effect. It is not wrong to want a large fee. However, it is unethical to take on a case when you are not competent to handle it. Of course, an attorney can often become competent by putting extra work into the case. The problem is that you will have to decide whether you can become competent without charging the client an unreasonable amount. Most attorneys will be overconfident that they can do so.

7. Because debt collection cases are often routine, the "script" might make an attorney fail to see ethical problems.

8. The attorney will believe he can be objective when cognitive biases make this difficult. A possible solution would be to consult with another attorney in your firm who is not involved with the case.

9. An outside law firm would be less likely to suffer from cognitive biases, such as ethical blindness, the halo effect, or the overconfidence effect.

10. Because the disclosure might not actually be adequate because of cognitive biases.

11. I'll leave this one to you.

12. Because their System 2 comes up with a rationalization for their System 1 actions. This helps us avoid cognitive dissonance between our idealized selves and our actual selves.

13. Ethical blindness and overconfidence effect. A lawyer may think he can be objective concerning both clients' interests, but his objectivity will break down when problems arise.

14. Since you know what answer your bosses want, it will be hard to be objective.

15. In this rule, the drafter is protecting lawyers from cognitive biases, regardless of whether the drafter knew specifically about cognitive biases. This rule helps an attorney overcome the overconfidence effect, which might cause an attorney to think that he could commingle client funds and personal funds without any ethical problems occurring.

II. Overcoming Legal Ethical Problems

Lawyers can use the techniques previously discussed in this book to overcome many ethical problems caused by cognitive biases (reflection, evaluation self-monitoring, practical reasoning, etc.). This section presents additional solutions and examples. Note: If many ethical failures are due to cognitive biases, rather than intentional conduct, then traditional punishments will have little effect on this conduct.

As I have discussed throughout this book, awareness of the bias alone can help eliminate the effect of many cognitive biases. For example, a study of distracted drivers demonstrated that mere awareness was very effective.[40] The author wrote, "In terms of attitudes that could produce a distracted driver, the researchers found that those who believed that the practice was either socially acceptable, or beyond their control, were more likely to self-identify as an offender." He continued, "One group of participants was asked to come up with a solution to stop dangerous driving behaviors (e.g., speeding) as they happened, while a control group was told the dangers of reckless driving, but not asked to formulate a prevention plan. Both groups saw similar declines in the incidence of distracted driving, which led the researchers to believe that merely completing the self-identifying survey and reviewing unsafe driving behaviors led to increased awareness."

Two scholars have created a seven-step process for dealing with legal ethical problems: "(1) framing the problem to be solved; (2) identifying and prioritizing values, interests, and objectives; (3) identifying and resolving major uncertainties concerning the cause of the problem; (4) generating a range of plausible solutions; (5) predicting the consequences of each course of action generated; (6) making a decision by selecting the course of action that optimizes interests and objectives; and (7) implementing, observing, and learning from the outcome of the decision."[41] The advantage of taking this approach is that it slows down your thinking. You will use System 2, rather than System 1.

Of course, education about cognitive biases, especially in law school, can help prevent future ethical problems. Behavioral legal ethicists believe that law schools should teach legal ethics in a new way, which reflects the new learning.[42] Two scholars have argued, "Behavioral ethics sees an opportunity in helping students and professionals better understand their own behavior in the ethics domain, and compare it to how they would ideally like to behave. We believe that only by reflecting on their ethical failures and the inconsistencies between their desire to be moral and their actual behavior they can rise to the actions (and ethical standards) that their more reflective selves would recommend."[43]

Professor Eldred described his legal ethics class, "The perspective I have taken over the last two years teaches behavioral science as a core aspect of my ethics class. The approach works on two tracks. The first integrates many of the central concepts from behavioral science into classroom discussions using a variety of techniques that have proven effective in other contexts to increase student engagement—such as participatory exercises that allow students to experience firsthand some of the illusions and cognitive biases well-documented in the behavioral research, role-plays and simulations to immerse students in some of the contextual and emotional dynamics that can influence ethical behavior, and the use of multimedia (especially video) that explore many of the core concepts in the area."[44] In addition, a "second track takes place outside of the classroom and focuses on a companion blog created for the course, entitled Understanding Behavioral Legal Ethics."

Another author has suggested that making ethics central to professional identity can help an attorney avoid lapses "when time and cognitive resources are in short supply."[45] This author added, "That is, one who puts great stock in having a positive moral identity is better equipped to resist the pull towards unethical conduct." This is another reason that law schools should include professional identity training in their curriculums.

Problem

Use the seven-step process to evaluate ethical problems that have recently arisen in your practice or you have read about.

Notes

1. Max H. Bazerman & Francesca Gino Toward a Deeper Understanding of Moral Judgment and Dishonesty, Annual Review of Law and Social Science [https://dash.harvard.edu/bitstream/handle/1/10996807/bazerman_gino_beh-ethics-toward_annual-review_dec2012.pdf]

2. Harvey S. James, Jr., *Why Do Good People Do Bad Things in Business? Lessons from Research for Responsible Business Managers*, at 5. [https://s3.amazonaws.com/academia.edu.documents/46206993/Why_Do_Good_People_Do_Bad_Things_in_Busi20160603-20832-pz8xvb.pdf?AWSAccessKeyId=AKIAIWOWYYGZ2Y53UL3A&Expires=1513115547&Signature=SnTgawrjYHOLaq4Tp88zrNST9P4%3D&response-content-disposition=inline%3B%20filename%3DWhy_Do_Good_People_Do_Bad_Things_in_Busi.pdf]

3. Bazerman & Gino, *supra* at 9.

4. Andrew M. Perlman, *A Behavioral Theory of Legal Ethics*, 90 IND. L.J. 1639 (2015); Jean R. Sternlight & Jennifer K. Robbennolt, *Behavioral Legal Ethics*, 45 ARIZ. ST. L.J. 1107 (2013).

5. By normative, I mean whether the conduct is morally acceptable.

6. Catherine Gage O'Grady, Behavioral Legal Ethics, Decision Making, and The New Attorney's Unique Professional Perspective, 15 NEVADA L.J. 671, 674 (2015) ("O'Grady 1).

7. *Id.* at 672.

8. Tigran W, Eldred, *Insights from Psychology: Teaching Behavioral Ethics as a Core Element of Professional Responsibility*, 2016 MICH. ST. L. REV. 757, 759 [HTTPS://DIGITALCOMMONS.LAW.MSU.EDU/CGI/VIEWCONTENT.CGI?REFERER=HTTPS://SCHOLAR.GOOGLE.COM/&HTTPSREDIR=1&ARTICLE=1171&CONTEXT=LR]

9. Bazerman & Gino, *supra* at 21.

10. O'Grady 1, *supra* at 674-75; Sternlight & Robbennolt, *supra at* 1111.

11. O'Grady 1, *supra*, at 679. One writer has noted, "There are two general explanations for why people engage in unethical behavior. The first explanation is that people desire evil and want to do bad things. A corollary is that evil acts are committed by evil people–that is, by people who inherently desire to inflict harm on others and whose satisfaction and well-being increase because others are harmed. This explanation cannot be fully discounted, since there are bad (even evil) people in this world. Nevertheless, this is a poor explanation for understanding business ethics problems in most contexts because character and behavior are infinitely complex." James, supra, at 6.

12. O'Grady 1, *supra* at 682.

13. Sternlight & Robbennolt, *supra* at 1117.

14. O'Grady, *supra* at 672; *see also* Eldred, *supra* at 766 ("situationism" "the general notion that the subtle aspects of a situation often play a significant role in how decisions are reached.").

15. Bazerman & Gino, *supra* at 14.

16. Sternlight & Robbennolt, *supra* at 1118.

17. Bazerman & Gino, *supra* at 17.

18. James, supra at 4.

19. Perlman, *supra* at 1649 (Several studies demonstrate that lawyers tend to offer different assessments of a case's value depending on which side the lawyers are asked to represent.").

20. Eldred, *supra* at 769.

21. *Id.* at 791-93; Sternlight & Robbennolt, *supra* at 1118.

22. O'Grady 1, *supra* at 679.

23. Sternlight & Robbennolt, *supra* at 1120-21.

24. *Id.* at 1121.

25. *Id.*

26. Catherine Gage O'Grady, *A Behavioral Approach to Lawyer Mistake and Apology*, 51 NEW ENGLAND L. REV. 7, 14 (2017). [https://papers.ssrn.com/sol3/papers.cfm?abstract_id=2848612] ("O'Grady 2")

27. *Id.* at 16-18.

28. *Id.* at 18.

29. *Id.* at 20-26.

30. *Id.* at 29-31.

31. Bazerman & Gino, *supra* at 23.

32. *Id.* at 1122.

33. *Id.* at 1122-23.

34. Bazerman & Gino, *supra* at 24.

35. Sternlight & Robbennolt, *supra*, at

36. James, supra, at 8.

37. Eldred, *supra*, at 793-94.

38. O'Grady 1, *supra*, at 682.

39. Robert Prentice, *Teaching Behavioral Ethics*, 31 J, Legal Studies Educ. 325, 331-32 (2014).

40. Study: Distracted Driving Worst Among Young Males, Extroverts, Neurotic People by Daniel Steingold Nov. 20, 2017. [https://www.studyfinds.org/distracted-driving-demographics-study/]

41. O'Grady 1, *supra*, at 676.

42. Perkman, *supra*, 1668; Eldred, *supra*; Prentice, *supra*.

43. Bazerman & Gino, *supra* at 32.

44. Eldred, *supra*, at 767.

45. Sternlight & Robbennolt, *supra* at 1161.

Chapter Eight
Special Topics

Chapter Goals.
1. To further develop the reader's ability to understand cognitive biases by showing how cognitive biases affect specific legal topics.
2. To show how cognitive biases affect the assessment of causation.
3. To introduce the reader to the narrative fallacy and the hindsight bias.
4. To discuss the dangers of what we do not know.
5. To examine cognitive biases and analogical fallacies.
6. To show the danger of turning off part of your brain.
7. To show the relationship of cognitive biases and legal persuasion.
8. To show how to avoid being persuaded by others who are using cognitive biases.
9. To examine juries and cognitive biases.
10. To show why traditional sexual harassment training is ineffective: cognitive biases.
11. To discuss a prosecutor's use of PowerPoint and cognitive biases.
12. To introduce a few more cognitive biases.
13. To discuss whether the government should set up policies to help people overcome cognitive biases.

In this chapter, I will demonstrate how cognitive biases work in specific areas.

I. Lack of Causal Connection: Illusory Correlation and Related Biases

Causation is an important concept in the law. Many lawyers try to find a causal connection where there is none. Illusory correlation: "Inaccurately perceiving a relationship between two unrelated events."[1]

One of the biggest defects in human thinking is finding a causal connection between two events when one does not exist. In other words, wrongly thinking that correlation equals causation. Under this bias, a person thinks that since B followed A, A must have caused B. This is not always true; one must prove A caused B.

We see correlation being confused with causation everyday. For example, after Superstorm Sandy, a number of politicians immediately blamed it on global warming. A prominent meteorologist criticized these politicians, stating that there was no evidence that global warming caused Sandy.[2]

A couple of years ago, there was a piece in the Washington Post by Professor Eugene Volokh on whether there is a correlation between state homicide rates and state gun laws.[3] After the terrible shooting in Oregon, many politicians clamored for more gun control laws in order to prevent similar tragic events. After comparing homicide rates to gun control ratings, Volokh concluded that there is zero correlation between the state homicide rate and state gun laws.

I have also been guilty of confusing correlation with causation. One evening, I started to have severe abdominal pains. I assumed that the pain was caused by food poisoning from the meal I had eaten that evening. When the pain didn't get better, I went to the emergency room, and I was told that I had an infected gall bladder.

Understanding and Overcoming Cognitive Biases for Lawyers and Law Students

The point of these stories is that you have to use System 2 to be an effective thinker concerning causation. Perform each step in the problem-solving process. Do not leave out a step, and do all steps thoroughly. In particular, you need to establish causation, rather than assuming it.

Examples.
I will use my lucky coin to scratch off my lottery ticket.
I do well on tests when I use my lucky pen.
When I wear my lucky tee shirt, my team wins.
Living in a big city makes people rude.
The full moon makes people crazy.
The Haitian earthquake was caused by global warming. (I read this one in the paper. No kidding.)
When I clicked my fingers, the whole city blacked out. I caused the great black out of 1968.
I always eat vegetable soup when I have a cold. Vegetable soup cures colds.

Here is an example of how a military instructor made a wrong decision based on a faulty analysis of causation.[4] The instructor observed that when his pilots did something bad and he yelled at them, they got better, but that when he praised them for doing something good, their performance got worse. He, therefore, concluded that he should only yell at his cadets. His problem was that he had confused causation with randomness. What he had observed had been "regression to the mean," "random fluctuations in the quality of performance." The praise or yelling had nothing to do with the performance. The good performances and the bad performances had just progressed to the mean. As Kahneman declared, "Causal explanation will be invoked when regression is detected, but they will be wrong because the truth is that regression to the mean has an explanation but does not have a cause."[5]

Of course, some connections are causal. Full moons do affect the severity of tides because of the gravitational pull of the moon.

Possible causes.
1. System 1 "infers and invents causes and intentions."[6]
2. Psychological heuristics: information processing shortcuts that underlie many human judgments, such as availability. "Hundreds of psychology studies have proven that we tend to overestimate the importance of events we can easily recall and underestimate the importance of events we have trouble recalling."[7]
3. "An information processing mechanism that assumes a noisy conversion of objective observations into subjective judgments. The theory defines noise as the mixing of these observations during retrieval from memory."
4. The need to create a coherent story.[8]
5. Limited working memory capacity.
6. Using limited information. For example, ignoring examples where there isn't a connection.

Trying to create a coherent story is the "narrative fallacy"–"flimsy accounts of the past that individuals believe are true."[9] This bias occurs because humans are continuously trying

Special Topics

to "make sense of the world."[10] In other words, humans connect unrelated events because it helps them make sense of a random world. Remember, System 1 likes things tidy.

The narrative fallacy can lead to the "hindsight bias–" the tendency to see past events as being predictable at the time those events happened."[11] This bias "leads observers to assess the quality of a decision not by whether the process was sound but whether its outcome was good or bad."[12]

Overcoming Illusory Correlation

1. Better understanding of causation.
2. Recognizing the possibility of randomness.
3. Carefully analyze whether a causal connection actually exists. This can be done through scientific experiments, statistical analysis, and thinking through (or writing out) all steps in a process.
4. Think of events that seem connected, but that are really random.
5. Think of several causal alternatives for an event, including randomness.

James Clear advocates using a contingency table to determine whether causation exists:[13]

	Hospital Admission	No Hospital Admission
Full Moon	A	B
No Full Moon	C	D

<u>Cell A</u>: Full moon and a busy night. This is a very memorable combination and is over-emphasized in our memory because it is easy to recall.
<u>Cell B</u>: Full moon, but nothing happens. This is a non-event and is under-emphasized in our memory because nothing really happened. It is hard to remember something not happening and we tend to ignore this cell.
<u>Cell C</u>: No full moon, but it is a busy night. This is easy to dismiss as a "crazy day at work."
<u>Cell D</u>: No full moon and a normal night. Nothing memorable happens on either end, so these events are easy to ignore as well.

Overcoming the Narrative Fallacy

1. Make sure you have all the facts.
2. Make sure you weigh the facts properly.
3. Ask whether you are letting your emotions affect your analysis.
4. Consider reasonable alternative interpretations.
5. Ask whether your interpretation is better than the alternatives.

Understanding and Overcoming Cognitive Biases for Lawyers and Law Students

Overcoming the Hindsight Bias

1. View events ex ante. (before the event)
2. Try to see events from the other person's viewpoint.

Exercises VIII-1

1. Think of times in your life when you confused correlation with causation. Were there any consequences?
2. Think of events in the news where politicians confused correlation with causation.
3. Think of sports events when an announcer confused randomness with causation.
4. Do you know about the concept of "winner's history"? Has does this relate to the narrative fallacy?
5. Can you think of how the narrative fallacy has been used by propagandists?
6. Have you ever been guilty of the hindsight bias?
7. Have you ever heard fans of a team criticizing the coach after the game is over? Think of other examples of the hindsight bias.
8. Have you ever blamed a doctor for making a wrong diagnosis ("hindsight bias")? Did the doctor have the same information when he made the diagnosis that you had afterwards?
11. Think about how a hindsight bias might affect a jury's deliberations. (A jury is more likely to find a defendant negligent in hindsight than foresight. This is also true for criminal defendants.) Is this unfair to the defendant? How can the defendant's attorney compensate for the hindsight bias?

Illusory causation can be the basis of other biases, such as in-group bias, the gambler's fallacy, and essentialism.

II. What We Do Not Know

A serious problem, related to our cognitive biases, is that humans often lack the knowledge to have a reasoned opinion or make a proper decision. As one article has recently asked, "How can so many people believe things that are demonstrably false?"[14] The authors continued, "But collective delusion is not new, nor is it the sole province of the political right. Plenty of liberals believe, counter to scientific consensus, that G.M.O.s are poisonous, and that vaccines cause autism."

The reason for this dilemma: "On their own, individuals are not well equipped to separate fact from fiction, and they never will be. Ignorance is our natural state; it is a product of the way the mind works." In other words, individuals lack the requisite knowledge to make decisions in many areas. (Even highly-intelligent people don't know everything.)

These authors believed that "What really sets human beings apart is not our individual mental capacity. The secret to our success is our ability to jointly pursue complex goals by dividing cognitive labor. . . . Each of us knows only a little bit, but together we can achieve remarkable feats." They added, "Knowledge isn't in my head or in your head. It's shared."

They give a couple of examples: "You know that the earth revolves around the sun.

Special Topics

But can you rehearse the astronomical observations and calculations that led to that conclusion? You know that smoking causes cancer. But can you articulate what smoke does to our cells, how cancers form and why some kinds of smoke are more dangerous than others? We're guessing no."

These authors noted, "One consequence of the fact that knowledge is distributed this way is that being part of a community of knowledge can make people feel as if they understand things they don't." Consequently, "The key point here is not that people are irrational; it's that this irrationality comes from a very rational place. People fail to distinguish what they know from what others know because it is often impossible to draw sharp boundaries between what knowledge resides in our heads and what resides elsewhere."

They continued, "This is especially true of divisive political issues. Your mind cannot master and retain sufficiently detailed knowledge about many of them. You must rely on your community. But if you are not aware that you are piggybacking on the knowledge of others, it can lead to hubris."

The authors concluded, "That individual ignorance is our natural state is a bitter pill to swallow. But if we take this medicine, it can be empowering. It can help us differentiate the questions that merit real investigation from those that invite a reactive and superficial analysis. It also can prompt us to demand expertise and nuanced analysis from our leaders, which is the only tried and true way to make effective policy. A better understanding of how little is actually inside our own heads would serve us well."

These authors also undertook a study of extreme political opinions about complex policies.[15] They concluded that these extreme positions are caused by simplistic causal models (conclusions drawn from limited evidence or understanding). They found that when researchers asked individuals to explain their opinions in depth in mechanistic terms, the individuals recognized their lack of understanding of the policies, and they adopted more moderate opinions.

I hope you can see how the above relates to our study of cognitive biases. Can you name the cognitive biases that relate to a lack of knowledge? [overconfidence effect, anchoring, availability heuristic, base-rate effect, essentialism, planning fallacy, normalcy bias, functional fixedness, halo effect, etc.]

When you hold an extreme position, ask yourself if you can explain the mechanistic basis of that opinion. (For example, what is your view on global warming, and why do you hold that view?) You should not rely on the overconfidence bias and related biases to allow unexamined thinking. An alternative approach is to write down the reasoning behind the position opposite to yours. When we understand the opinions of others better, we understand our opinions better.

Problem

Think about how the lack of knowledge to have a reasoned opinion or make a proper decision can affect a lawyer. First, consider the lawyer's duty of competence. Also, consider how many malpractice suits arise. Anything else?

III. Analogical Fallacies

Understanding and Overcoming Cognitive Biases for Lawyers and Law Students

One way humans think is by analogies. In fact, reasoning by analogies is a major type of legal reasoning. A is like B in a certain way, so other aspects of A are like other aspects of B. Here is a more detailed definition:

> An analogy is a comparison between two objects, or systems of objects, that highlights respects in which they are thought to be similar. Analogical reasoning is any type of thinking that relies upon an analogy. An analogical argument is an explicit representation of a form of analogical reasoning that cites accepted similarities between two systems to support the conclusion that some further similarity exists. . . . Analogical reasoning is fundamental to human thought.[16]

Here is how legal analogies work: The facts (or reasoning) of case A are like the facts or reasoning of case B, so the rule from case A applies to case B.

An analogical argument is often used to support a conclusion, as in 3-5 below.

Examples.
1. Coffee is to a coffee pot as tea is to a tea pot. (Coffee is brewed in a coffee pot; tea is brewed in a tea pot.)
2. Day is to night as right is to wrong. (Day is opposite of night; right is opposite of wrong.)
3. My child likes ice cream. Frozen yogurt is like ice cream, so my child will like frozen yogurt.
4. Transgendered persons are like gays, so the law should treat transgendered persons like gays.
5. Alpha 4 has an atmosphere similar to Earth's so Alpha 4 can support life.

Extended examples.
"In 1934, the pharmacologist Schaumann was testing synthetic compounds for their antispasmodic effect. These drugs had a chemical structure similar to morphine. He observed that one of the compounds—meperidine, also known as Demerol—had a physical effect on mice that was previously observed only with morphine: it induced an S-shaped tail curvature. By analogy, he conjectured that the drug might also share morphine's narcotic effects. Testing on rats, rabbits, dogs and eventually humans showed that meperidine, like morphine, was an effective pain-killer."[17]
Scientists recently discovered a planet orbiting around a star, which is similar to our Sun. The planet is the same distance from its star as Earth is from the Sun. The planet's atmosphere contains oxygen. Conclusion: The new planet may support life.

The key to reasoning by analogy is the closeness of the similarity. The more similar the items, the more likely the analogy will be accepted.

Here are some of the traits that make analogies stronger and weaker:

Special Topics

"The more similarities (between two domains), the stronger the analogy.
The more differences, the weaker the analogy.
The greater the extent of our ignorance about the two domains, the weaker the analogy.
The weaker the conclusion, the more plausible the analogy.
Analogies involving causal relations are more plausible than those not involving causal relations.
Structural analogies are stronger than those based on superficial similarities.
The relevance of the similarities and differences to the conclusion (i.e., to the hypothetical analogy) must be taken into account.
Multiple analogies supporting the same conclusion make the argument stronger."[18]

A false analogy occurs when two things are similar in one way but not in material (key) aspects.

Cognitive biases can affect how humans perceive the similarities in analogies. For example, the availability heuristic can affect how we view analogies. Say, you are trying to sell your cell phone service. Company A is the standard in the cell phone industry. You work for Company B. Your ad: "Our cell phone service covers 99% of the area that Company A's service does, but we cost half as much." The analogy in the above is that Company B has almost the same coverage as Company A, so the service from both companies is about the same. But, is service area the only factor in choosing a cell carrier? How about reliability? Features? Band width? So Company B is using the availability heuristic to sell its service by leaving out information.

Faulty analogies can similarly involve essentialism and in-group thinking. Can you think of any other biases that might affect analogies?

Finally, emotionally-laden analogies trigger our System 1s. Is this a good analogy? "The environmental movement is like Naziism."

How might the confirmation bias relate to faulty analogies?

Overcoming Faulty Analogies Involving Cognitive Biases

1. Examine the analogy carefully. What is its purpose (context)?
2. What are the similarities? Are they convincing?
3. Has any material information been left out?

Problem

Proposition: Ideas spread in an evolutionary manner just like genes spread. (memetic theory). Examine the analogy in this proposition. Is it convincing? How might cognitive biases be involved? (Feel free to look up meme theory on the net.)

IV. **Turning Off Part of Your Brain**

A recent study has shown that under certain circumstances humans turn off parts of their brains. For example, when someone uses satellite navigation to find a destination, they turn off the part of the brain that considers alternative routes.[19]

"Previous UCL research has shown that the hippocampi of London taxi drivers expand as they learn 'the Knowledge', memorising the streets and landmarks of central London. The latest study suggests that drivers who follow satnav directions do not engage their hippocampus, likely limiting any learning of the city street network."[20]

"The study, published in Nature Communications and funded by Wellcome, involved 24 volunteers navigating a simulation of Soho in central London while undergoing brain scans. The researchers investigated activity in the hippocampus, a brain region involved in memory and navigation, and the prefrontal cortex which is involved in planning and decision-making. They also mapped the labyrinth of London's streets to understand how these brain regions reacted to them." According to the article, "When volunteers navigated manually, their hippocampus and prefrontal cortex had spikes of activity when volunteers entered new streets. This brain activity was greater when the number of options to choose from increased, but no additional activity was detected when people followed satnav instructions."

Although an isolated study, the above has enormous consequences for the understanding of brain biases. We have seen that when System 1 receives some information, it shuts down to other alternatives. This occurs with anchoring, the availability heuristic, the bandwagon effect, the base-rate effect, the bias blind spot, etc.

The implication of the above is that we must always force ourselves to focus on the alternatives and must not let a gps force us in only one of the possible directions.

Problems

1. Think of other ways that technology might be hurting the development of human thinking and learning? I'll give you one–using a calculator rather than doing the math in your head.
2. Think of ways in which shutting off part of your brain might affect your law practice. Brainstorm. I'll give you one. Relying exclusively on Lexis or a similar service for legal research.

V. Cognitive Biases and Legal Persuasion

Many of you have already probably realized that cognitive biases can be used for persuasion. For example, advertisers have been using cognitive biases for many years to sell their products. They use framing, emotional reasoning, incomplete information (the availability heuristic), anchoring, hyperbolic discounting, etc., to sell their products. Based on your training in cognitive biases in previous chapters, you should be able to identify cognitive biases used by advertisers.

Advertising Exercises

See if you can spot the problems in the following ads.

Special Topics

1. Buy now, and you won't have to pay for six months.
2. Buy our sneakers. Famed basketball player Larry Jordan endorsed our brand.
3. Sure, our widgets are a little more expensive, but doesn't your family deserve the best?
4. Our cell phone service covers 99% of the area that our competitor's does, yet it costs 25% less per month.
5. Everybody's buying a Yugo. How about you?
6. Our dresses are marked at 10% off.
7. Dora came to our hospital after her accident. She was lucky because we have the best neurologists in town.
8. An ad that tries to get your to devote to a charity by telling the story of a sick young boy.
9. Eat healthy! Eat our sandwiches at our restaurant because they contain lots of veggies.
10. If you have an accident, will you get the full value of your car. At most insurance companies; they take off for depreciation. Not at the Happy Insurance Company. We give you what you paid for your car, even if the accident was your fault.
11. An ad that makes smoking look cool from before warning labels.
12. We put msg in our food because you're worth it.
13. Playing an ad on television again and again.
14. We fill our bottles 7/8 to the top. Our competitors leave their bottles 1/8 empty.
15. A car speeding down a scenic highway.
16. A juicy burger in a restaurant ad.
17. You can drive a luxury car at an affordable price.
18. Call now. Our product is only available for the next hour.
19. We asked five people in a blind test whether they preferred our swamp water or the most expensive bottled water. Four out of five preferred our swamp water.

Comment

1. The price will be the same in six months; in fact, the seller will probably charge more to compensate by charging more for the delay in getting its money. However, most consumers like the buy now, pay later term because it fits with their cognitive biases. (A variation on hyperbolic discounting)
2. This is a clear example of the halo effect. The fact that Larry Jordan endorsed them says nothing about the quality of the shoe. People often pay many times the actual value of a product because it is endorsed by a celebrity.
3. The ad is trying to get you to buy their product based on your System 1 emotions.
4. This is an example of narrow framing. How do the other aspects of the cell services compare? Reliability? Features? Etc.
5. Bandwagon effect.
6. Anchoring effect.
7. You have probably seen many ads like this. A hospital is trying to show that it is the one you should use by preying on your emotions. It wants you to think "wow, she might have died if she has gone to any other hospital." This is an example of an ad that tries to create an availability heuristic or anchoring. You should choose the best hospital based on research and what your pcp recommends, not on an ad. Nevertheless, some hospitals continue to run these

types of ads.
8. The identifiable-victim effect.
9. Framing. Everyone wants to eat healthy, right? But, what else is on the sandwiches? Fatty meat? Mayonnaise? What else are you eating at the restaurant? Chips? Sugary drinks?
10. This could work. However, you do realize that your rates will be much higher under this kind of policy. You get what you pay for. Look at the transaction closely. Don't let the framing fool you.
11. Framing effect and several others. Ignores health risks of smoking.
12. Appealing to your emotions again.
13. Trying to create the mere-exposure effect.
14. Framing effect.
15. Framing effect. The picture sets the frame.
16. Same thing.
17. Notice the loaded words (luxury and affordable).
18. Yeah, I bet. The ad is playing with your emotions.
19. Beware of small sample sizes.

Law schools teach their students persuasive writing during their first year. As one writer has noted, lawyers persuade "using various rhetorical techniques, attempting to manage other people's perceptions of such things as the facts, the lawyer's own theory of the case, the credibility of eyewitness testimony, the weaknesses of opposing counsel's claims, and the praiseworthiness of the lawyer's own client."[21] The author continued: "For the art of persuasion is intimately connected with the psychological process of perception."[22] In other words, most of the persuasive techniques law schools taught you were based on cognitive biases.

You were taught that you should phrase issues in a persuasive document from your client's viewpoint. This is an example of framing. It has often been said that the attorney who can get the judge to accept her framing of the issue will win the case.

Examples.
Has a contract been made when one of the parties is legally drunk?
Has a contract been made when one of the parties is legally drunk, but the other party is not aware that the first party is drunk?

The first example uses the availability heuristic; it leaves out information that might hurt the case. The other example fills in the missing information so it is persuasive for the otherside.

Did the steel company breach the contract when it delivered AC-5 steel because AC-6 steel was specified in the contact?
Did the steel company satisfy the contract when it delivered AC-5 steel since AC-5 steel is the same as AC-6 steel in all material aspects?

Facts are also written to be persuasive.

Special Topics

Examples.
Jonathan, an alter boy at his church, was not aware that his friend was going to rob the store.

In this example, the author appeals to your emotions by describing Jonathan as an alter boy, and it uses the halo effect. This helps set up the important second half of the sentence.

Assume this example is about a coerced confession:
The police officer slammed the defendant against the car.
The police officer pushed the defendant against the car, after he tried to escape.

Word choice is key in these examples. In the first version, "slammed" is a loaded word intended to invoke an emotional reaction in the reader. The second version uses a neutral word, and it includes additional details that soften the first part of the sentence.

We can also look at persuasion from the view point of the techniques being employed.

1. Information presented first and last is more likely to be remembered.
2. The level of detail affects how likely something will be remembered.
3. Word choice affects persuasion.
4. Sentence structure can affect persuasion.
5. Personalize your client. Depersonalize your opponent.
6. Emphasize favorable information.
7. De-emphasize unfavorable information.
8. Use emotions.

All of these persuasive devices involve cognitive biases.

One of the things that you were taught in legal writing was that the reader was more likely to remember information presented first and last. The first part involves cognitive biases like the anchor bias and availability heuristic. Likewise, because these biases cause you to remember information you received first, the confirmation bias, expectation bias, and the Semmelweis reflex are also involved since they reinforce your initial conclusion. The availability heuristic explains why we remember the things we heard last, rather than things in the middle.

Level of detail affects persuasiveness because detail focuses our mind on information (availability heuristic). On the other hand, when a writer presents something quickly the reader will probably soon forget it in favor of the detailed information. Likewise, a writer uses level of detail in connection with the confirmation bias.

As we have seen before, word choice affects framing. A writer should use the best word (most exact meaning) to persuade the reader. Similarly, a word can have the same meaning, but a different emotional connotation. Ex. Slammed v. pushed, demanded v. asked, told v. ordered.

Sentence structure can influence persuasion by drawing or deflecting attention from information. Use of the passive voice de-emphasizes or hides the actor. Ex. The Governor made mistakes. (active) v. Mistakes were made by the Governor. (passive, de-emphasizes the actor) v. Mistakes were made. (passive, hides the actor). Similarly, using compound versus complex sentence structure can change emphasis. An idea in an independent clause usually receives more stress than an idea in a dependant clause.[23] A compound sentence contains two or more independent clauses. A complex sentence contains an independent clause and a dependent clause. Ex. Although she ran the stop sign, defective brakes caused the accident. In this sentence, I de-emphasized ran the stop sign and emphasized defective brakes caused the accident by putting the first part in a dependent clause and the second part in an independent clause. In other words, I am trying to focus the reader's attention on the good information, rather than the bad. Ex. The criminal had blood on his face, and he tested negative for gun powder residue. A writer might want to change this compound sentence structure to complex sentence structure depending on the side she represents. The defendant had blood on his face, although he tested negative for gun powder residue. v. While the defendant had blood on his face, he tested negative for gun powder residue. In sum, sentence structure allows you to be honest with the court, while still presenting your client's best case. And, all this is due to cognitive biases.

In the 1980 New York Senate race, Republican candidate, Rick Lazio, kept referring to his opponent as "my opponent" in a series of campaign ads. Who was his opponent? Hillary Clinton. His strategy of depersonalizing her didn't win him the election, but it still was an effective strategy. In persuasive writing, a lawyer should personalize his client and depersonalize his opponent. Why does this strategy work–the identifiable victim effect.

Emphasizing favorable information uses techniques I have already discussed. Put favorable facts first and last. Give favorable facts more detail, more room. Use word choice. Do the opposite with unfavorable information. Hide it in the middle of an argument. Hide it in the middle of a paragraph or sentence. Give it little detail. Use neutral language.

The final persuasive technique is using emotions. As we have seen throughout this book, emotion can turn off the reasoned judgment of System 2. But, be cautious. You can overdo it. Also, an appeal to the emotions is more effective in some sections of a brief than others. Can you think of which section it would be most effective in?

Other persuasive techniques.
1. Using loaded language with a witness immediately after the occurrence.[24] (This one is bad because it influences a witnesses memory.)
2. "When separate pieces of evidence are presented one at a time, rather than all at once, the evidence is perceived to be stronger."[25]
3. Negativity themes have more impact on a judge than positive ones.[26]
4. Don't let the otherside frame the issues, the evidence, or the facts.

A final question is whether using cognitive biases for persuasion is ethical. As we have seen, cognitive biases are used by advertisers, politicians, and many others to persuade. Sometimes these groups go overboard in their use of cognitive biases. What about lawyers?

The purpose of a court proceeding is to get at the truth. However, truth is often not easy to find. This is especially true in an adversary system like we have in the United States.

As long as we continue to use an adversary system to adjudicate disputes, we must

Special Topics

allow lawyers to use persuasion. But, since we still must get at the truth, we should limit persuasion to a *reasonable* presentation of the case. In other words, anything that is likely to prevent getting at the truth should be unethical.

And, oh boy! We're back to reasonable again. Can an attorney objectively tell whether she has presented a "reasonable" view of her case? The one check on this is that a neutral judge is presiding over the case, and the attorney is subject to the ethical rules. Maybe this is the best we can do in an adversarial system. Since the human reasoning process is not perfect, we will probably not be able to place restraints that make the system perfect.

Reflection Questions

1. How important are persuasive techniques in convincing a judge?
2. Can you see how cognitive biases are the foundation for persuasiveness?
3. Think how particular persuasive techniques match up with particular cognitive biases.

Problems

1. There is a great deal of debate among legal writing professors as to whether an appellant should raise the appellee's arguments with counter arguments in the original brief or wait for the reply brief. Can you think of a reason based on cognitive biases why the first option might be preferable?
2. Look at a persuasive document you have recently written. How persuasive is the document? Is the issue persuasive? Are the facts persuasive? Is the summary of the argument persuasive? Are the point headings persuasive? Is the argument persuasive? How did you use cognitive biases in the above sections (whether you realized it or not)? Be critical–did you over do it anywhere? How could you have written the document better if you had been more aware of cognitive biases?

Answers

1. If you present your counter arguments in the initial brief, you get your ideas to the judges first, which means they will be more likely to accept them (anchor bias, availability heuristic, confirmation bias). Of course, there is a danger that you will suggest arguments to the otherside. Accordingly, I tell students to present their counter arguments in the initial brief unless the argument is a creative one, which the otherside might not make.

VI. Avoiding Being Persuaded by Cognitive Biases

In my previous book on cognitive biases, I showed how companies are manipulating consumers and their employees by using cognitive biases. For example, the New York Times published an article on how Uber uses cognitive psychology to manipulate its drivers.[27] The article declares, "And yet even as Uber talks up its determination to treat drivers more humanely, it is engaged in an extraordinary behind-the-scenes experiment in behavioral science to manipulate them in the service of its corporate growth . . ." A week after the New York

Times article, 60 Minutes had a story on how smartphones and social media are "brain hacking."[28] When you check your phone, it's like playing a slot machine because the user sometimes gets a reward. A tech company head similarly declared, "You're guinea pigs. You are guinea pigs in the box pushing the button and sometimes getting the likes. And they're doing this to keep you in there." "The longer we look at our screens, the more data companies collect about us, and the more ads we see. Ad spending on social media has doubled in just two years to more than $31 billion." Finally, there is even a guidebook for companies that want to manipulate their customers to buy more–*Hooked: How to Build Habit Forming Products*, by Nir Eyal with Ryan Hoover (2014).

The best way to avoid being manipulated by others is to be aware of cognitive biases. Avoiding them should be part of your everyday thought processes. Slow down. Use your System 2, instead of your System 1. Don't make snap decisions about important matters. Don't be a lazy thinker. Use the techniques mentioned earlier in this book: reflection, self-monitoring, evaluation, self-monitoring, practical reason.

Here are some solutions to specific cognitive biases:

1. Watch for illusory correlation–lack of causation in your opponent's arguments. Check these arguments carefully to see whether the otherside has established all connections, or whether they are just assuming causation.
2. There are three methods someone may use to reduce cognitive dissonance: "(I) discount the importance of conflicting cognitions to maintain the status quo, (2) add new cognitions that justify the behavior or belief, (3) or change the behavior or belief."[29]
3. Don't let yourself be manipulated by economic biases. Rely on probability, rather than intuition.

VII. Juries and Cognitive Biases

Jurors are subject to cognitive biases, just like everyone else. They will bring cognitive biases to the courtroom, and both sides will try to persuade the jury with cognitive biases, even if they are not aware of what cognitive biases are.

Here are some biases that you need to be careful with when dealing with a jury:

1. Curse of knowledge bias. Never assume that the jury knows what you know. Talk slowly. Carefully explain everything to the jury, without talking down to them. Do everything you can to help the jury understand your case, such as the use of exhibits. Educate the jury!!! Also, be careful with your experts and the curse of knowledge bias.
2. Empathy gap and projection bias. Don't assume that the jury is feeling what you feel. You may feel great sympathy for your client, but remember you will have worked with her for several months. It will take more to get the jury to sympathize with your client.
3. In-group bias. Juries today are diverse. Try to get the jury to be a part of your in-group. "We are all New Yorkers."
4. A defendant's attorney needs to strategize against the hindsight bias. The jury may think your client could have easily have avoided the improper conduct because of the hindsight bias.

Special Topics

Try to make the jury see the conduct as your client did, before or during the action. (See below)
5. Use the identifiable victim effect when possible.
6. Be able to explain economic biases to the jury.
7. Mind reading. Don't assume you know the jurors' thoughts.
8. Don't be an ostrich. Meet all the problems in your case head-on.
9. Don't suffer from subjective validation. You may hate your opponent, but don't let that hurt your case. I was once at a trial where both sides were trying to show how awful the otherside's client was. Both attorneys barely touched on the real issues.
10. A big problem with all people, including jurors, is that they make decisions early in the case. Then, they suffer from the confirmation bias as the case goes on this. This tells you a lot on how you should present your case to a jury.

Here is an example of how to deal with a hindsight bias and jurors. An engineer and architect designed a tall building to withstand 125 mph winds. The building collapsed in 150 mph winds. Were the designers negligent? The hindsight bias and outcome bias could lead the jury to think that they were. However, let's view this from the time they were designing the building. Local laws required that buildings be designed to withstand 125 mph winds, and no other building in the area was designed to survive 130 mph winds. Moreover, there had never been a recorded wind in the area over 100 mph. Finally, protecting the building against 150 mph winds would have add an additional third to the cost of the building. Were the designers negligent?

Here's another one. An expert witness (a radiologist) testifies that the defendant should have seen the tumor based on an early ex-ray. But, didn't the expert have an advantage because he already knew the tumor was there?

Consider how the hindsight bias might affect legal malpractice.

Watch out for your opponent's use of cognitive biases:

1. Using an improper anchor or base-rate. Your knowledge of cognitive biases can help you spot the opposing attorney's improper or dishonest reasoning. Make sure the jury has the proper methods to analyze all aspects of a case.
2. Using an in-group bias. This one can particularly hurt your case. Never let your opponent label you client or you as an outsider. Don't let the attorney label her client as an insider.
3. Watch out for bandwagon effect. Don't let the opposing attorney put his client on the bandwagon.
4. Emotional reasoning is an important part of most jury trials. Be ready to counter your opponent's use of emotional reasoning.
5. Watch for the framing effect. The attorney who frames the issues her way usually wins the case.
6. Don't allow your opponent to create causation between two things or events when there is none.
7. Watch for information overload. Overload causes jurors to use heuristics.

Understanding and Overcoming Cognitive Biases for Lawyers and Law Students

Pointer: Voir dire is a great opportunity to test jurors concerning their cognitive biases and to lay the foundation to overcome them. Remember jurors filter what they hear based on their knowledge and experiences so it is very important to realize who each juror is.

A key question is whether you should use cognitive biases when dealing with juries. The answer is you have no choice. But, remember that there is an opposing attorney who will pounce on your errors and a judge whose job it is to keep the proceeding fair. They may not know as much as you about cognitive biases, but they will usuakky realize when you are trying to pull something over on the jury.

Problems

1. Why is it better to use a motion in limne, rather than make evidentiary objections at trial?
2. Consider how the anchor bias and base-rate effect can influence the size of jury verdicts. How do statutory maximums affect the size of jury verdicts?
3. Consider the same factors with sentencing. How do minimum sentence statutes affect the ultimate sentence?
4. Why do you think judges often limit pretrial publicity?
5. There has been a lot in the news recently about sexual harassment. How do you think this might influence a juror trying a sexual harassment case?
6. How does the hindsight bias influence the size of punitive damages awards?
7. What is the most important question to ask during voir dire in a trial concerning sexual harassment?
8. Why can having smart people on a jury sometimes be dangerous?
9. Should judges consider cognitive biases when framing jury instructions?
10. Which are better to use with jurors statistical predictions or clinical predictions?
11. Is it better for a criminal defendant to have a jury trial or to be tried by a judge?
12. Why do judges sometimes prohibit pretrial publicity?

Answers

1. Because it is hard for someone to unhear something because of biases like the confirmation bias or the availability heuristic.
5. This involves the availability heuristic. Jurors might be more likely to find for the plaintiff in a sexual harassment case because they think it occurs so much.
7. Do you know anyone who has been sexually harassed? Availability heuristic.
8. Curse of knowledge bias. Availability heuristic.
12. Availability heuristic.

How are judges like jurors concerning cognitive biases? For example, how might a judge be affected by a confirmation bias? An anchor bias? A base-rate fallacy?

VIII. Cognitive Biases and Sexual Harassment Training

Special Topics

Recently, there has been an avalanche of stories on sexual harassment by politicians, actors, directors, college professors, and classical conductors. Along with these stories have come calls for sexual harassment training, even for Congress. This is a very important problem for lawyers. The solution to prevent sexual harassment lawsuits usually suggested by lawyers is sexual harassment training. However, many studies have shown that traditional sexual harassment training doesn't work.[30] Can anything be done to fix sexual harassment training? Is sexual harassment training for employees an effective deterrent for lawsuits?

The problem with current sexual harassment training is that attendees are taught what sexual harassment is; they are not taught how to recognize it in themselves. Three kinds of people attend sexual harassment training: 1) those who don't need it because they already know how to act like human beings, 2) those who realize what they are doing and don't care, and 3) those who think sexual harassment is wrong but don't recognize that they are sexual harassers. Sexual harassment training will not help those in group 2. What members of this group need to curtail their misconduct is the threat of punishment and public embarrassment. Sexual harassment training, however, can help those in group 3, but only if they are shown that "cognitive biases" are preventing them from recognizing that they are sexual harassers.

Does the above sound familiar? It is the same type of analysis I used in connection with behavioral legal ethics: Many sexual harassers are not bad people; they are just ethically blind to their harassment. Under this bias, a person can find sexual harassment to be repugnant, but that person can still commit sexual harassment himself because he doesn't recognize that his conduct is sexual harassment because of the bias. For example, a comedian might think that grabbing a sleeping woman's breasts is not sexual harassment because it is funny. However, the comedian never considered how the victim would feel. Similarly, a boss might not recognize that touching an employee in the wrong place is sexual harassment because he thinks it is just touching.

Another type of cognitive bias that affects sexual harassment is the overconfidence effect. Under this bias in relation to sexual harassment, a person is overconfident that he can act ethically in a certain situation. However, this objective predication is affected by emotions and the context of the event. As I noted in the last chapter, humans are often guilty of faulty emotional predictions. We think that we will act in a certain way when something happens, but we don't account for the effects of our emotions and how the situation influences them. For example, a law professor may objectively believe that he can have an affair with one of his students without crossing ethical boundaries. However, when trouble arises in the relationship, the emotions created by the situation that produced the trouble often results in a sexual harassment suit.

Another problem with sexual harassment is the "slippery slope." This begins with minor infractions that lead to more serious ones. For example, a boss may believe that touching a female employee's hand is okay. He then moves on to more serious things–massaging her shoulders, putting a hand on her thigh, etc. Then, he does serious kinds of sexual harassment without realizing he is acting improperly.

Finally, a person may have a script for how to handle situations that might involve sexual harassment. When something is not on that script, he doesn't recognize the problem as a possible sexual harassment situation, and a violation may occur. For example, a man might have scripted ways to avoid sexual harassment situations at work, but not at office parties.

Understanding and Overcoming Cognitive Biases for Lawyers and Law Students

How can new and improved sexual harassment training help an individual overcome these cognitive biases? First, the training must make the attendees aware of the cognitive biases that affect sexual harassment. Second, the training must teach participants to self-reflect. Not to just learn the rules, but to think about what the rules mean and why they exist. Not to just be aware of the cognitive biases, but to think about how they might affect the individual's behavior. A particularly effective type of reflection is to put yourself in the other person's shoes. With sexual harassment, a person should think about how the victim will feel about the misconduct. Most humans are very empathetic, but they sometimes need to be shown situations in which empathy is needed. Third, role playing can be a very effective method of overcoming cognitive biases. Fourth, when in doubt, an individual should consult a neutral third party. Finally, slow down! A lot of sexual harassment occurs when the individual is acting based on intuition. Slow, reasoned judgment can help you avoid misconduct in many situations.

An important question concerning sexual harassment in the workplace is why management and fellow workers don't help those who have been sexually harassed. For example, Wired published an article, entitled Many Startup Founders Doubt Extent of Sexual Harassment by Erin Griffith.[31] The article stated, "a new survey conducted by venture firm First Round Capital suggests that startup founders still have a long way to go when it comes to acknowledging and addressing the problem. The survey polled more than 800 startup founders, 17 percent of whom identified as female. According to the survey, more than half of startup founders have experienced or know someone who has experienced sexual harassment in the workplace. A full 78 percent of the women surveyed answered yes to the question." "Yet 19 percent of respondents said the problem of sexual harassment in tech has been overblown by the media; men were four times more likely to say this than women."

A large part of the answer is that cognitive biases make people unaware of what is happening around them. As two behavioral ethics scholars have written, "People are often unaware of the unethical conduct around them."[32] In other words, they suffer from a type of ethical blindness.

Other types of cognitive biases are also at work here. First, under the overconfidence effect, bosses think that they can avoid sexual harassment problems at their firms, even if other companies have problems. Second, the boss may be suffering from a lack of information bias, such as the availability heuristic. Third, under the bias blind spot, bosses can fail to see their own biases. Related to this, a boss may fail to see harassment charges against a member of her own group. Fourth, under the halo effect where people judge an individual based on a dominant characteristic such as looks, the bosses fail to see that their smartest employees might have character flaws. Finally, the bandwagon effect may preclude outrage at popular or important employees.

You can also analyze this question using Rest's four capacities: (1) moral sensitivity (or moral awareness), 2) moral reasoning (or judgment), 3) moral motivation, and 4) moral implementation (or moral courage). I have already discussed the problem with moral sensitivity above. People are often unaware of what's happening around them because of ethical blindness, the overconfidence effect, the halo effect, etc. As I wrote in Chapter Six, you can improve your ethical sensitivity by paying more attention to the world around you, instead of putting your head in the sand (ostrich effect). You should also <u>reflect</u> on what is happening around you and consider the effect of emotions on your sensitivity. The moral reasoning prong is fairly simple for this problem. When you consider the alternatives, punishing the harasser and helping the harassed is the right thing to do. Moral motivation requires that you overcome your self interest, such as any friendship with the harasser. How important are your intrinsic values?

Moral courage is the hardest factor for this problem. Standing up to a harasser is difficult. The harasser will often be a type A man who is difficult to deal with, and many people fear conflict and crave acceptance. Standing up to the harasser means that you will have to overcome your negativity biases. You will also have to stand up to those in your organization–your superiors and your colleagues. You will feel a great deal of peer pressure (the bandwagon effect). The accused might be very popular due to the halo effect. Your bosses and co-workers may also want to avoid conflict (self-interest and negativity biases). Finally, you will be influenced by what might happen to your career (what if); you will be known as a whistle-blower for the rest of your life. Having the moral courage to do the right thing can be hard, but, if you have empathy for the victim, you can do it.

Reflect on these questions: How many children would have been spared from physical and psychological harm if someone had stood up to the Penn State coach early on? Ask the same question for the Olympic gymnasts. What about Harvey Weinstein's victims? In other words, the harm caused by standing up to a harasser is much less than letting him continue his harassment.

Problem

I came up with this analysis of the causes of sexual harassment by analogy with the bases of behavioral legal ethics. I saw that a major cause of legal ethical lapses was ethical blindness. By studying sexual harassment, I concluded that a major cause of sexual harassment was similarly ethical blindness. Can you think of any other legal or societal problem that is also caused by ethical blindness? Brainstorm, and you will start to see how much cognitive biases affect our professional and personal lives.

IX. Prosecutor's Use of PowerPoint

From the Marshall Project:[33]

At least 10 times in the last two years, U.S. courts have reversed a criminal conviction because prosecutors violated the rules of fair argument with PowerPoint. In even more cases, an appellate court has taken note of such misconduct while upholding the conviction anyway or while reversing on other grounds. Legal watchdogs have long asserted that prosecutors have plenty of ways to quietly put their thumb on the scales of justice—such as concealing exculpatory evidence, eliminating jury-pool members based on race, and so on. Now they can add another category: prosecution by PowerPoint. "It's the classic 'A picture is worth a thousand words,'" said Eric Broman, a Seattle attorney who focuses on criminal appeals. "Until the courts say where the boundaries are, prosecutors will continue to test the boundaries."

Perhaps the most common misuse of what some legal scholars call "visual advocacy"

Understanding and Overcoming Cognitive Biases for Lawyers and Law Students

is the emblazoning of the word "Guilty" across a defendant's photo. Almost always the letters are red—the "color of blood and the color used to denote losses," as one court wrote.

1. What cognitive biases are involved in the above?
2. Can the manner of presentation unduly influence a jury? Can you think of other examples?
3. Should courts also limit how criminal defendants present a case? What about in civil trials?
4. Can visual aids help a jury understand a case?
5. Where and how should the court set the limits?
6. Can you think of other technologies that might assert undue influence over a jury?

X. Additional Biases

Here are a few biases I have not mentioned previously.[34] Consider whether they have ever affected your thinking. Even if they haven't, give examples of each and consider ways to overcome them using the list. Also, think about how they relate to the other biases we have discussed earlier.

1. Clustering illusion: "This is the tendency to see patterns in random events. It is central to various gambling fallacies, like the idea that red is more or less likely to turn up on a roulette table after a string of reds."
2. Fundamental-attribution error: "This is where you attribute a person's behavior to an intrinsic quality of her identity rather than the situation she's in. For instance, you might think your colleague is an angry person, when she is really just upset because she stubbed her toe."
3. Irrational escalation: "When people make irrational decisions based on past rational decisions. It may happen in an auction, when a bidding war spurs two bidders to offer more than they would other be willing to pay."
4. Outcome bias: "Judging a decision based on the outcome—rather than how exactly the decision was made in the moment. Just because you won a lot in Vegas doesn't mean gambling your money was a smart decision."
5. Placebo effect: "When simply believing that something will have a certain impact on you causes it to have that effect. This is a basic principle of stock market cycles, as well as a supporting feature of medical treatment in general. People given 'fake' pills often experience the same physiological effects as people given the real thing."
6. Illusory-truth effect: "A tendency to believe that a statement is true if it is easier to process, or if it has been stated multiple times, regardless of its actual veracity."
7. Insensitivity to sample size: "The tendency to underexpect variation in small samples."
8. Neglect of probability: "The tendency to completely disregard probability when making a decision under uncertainty."
9. Omission bias: "The tendency to judge harmful actions as worse, or less moral, than equally harmful omissions (inactions)."
10. Authority bias: "The tendency to attribute greater accuracy to the opinion of an authority figure (unrelated to its content) and be more influenced by that opinion."
11. False-consensus effect: "The tendency for people to overestimate the degree to which others agree with them."

Special Topics

12. Just-world hypothesis: "The tendency for people to want to believe that the world is fundamentally just, causing them to rationalize an otherwise inexplicable injustice as deserved by the victim(s)."

13, Naïve realism: "The belief that we see reality as it really is – objectively and without bias; that the facts are plain for all to see; that rational people will agree with us; and that those who don't are either uninformed, lazy, irrational, or biased."

IV. Should the Government Set Policies to Help Its Citizens Overcome Cognitive Biases?

Question

1. Should the government set policies to encourage citizens to overcome their cognitive biases?

Comment

1. You should think about this question deeply. In 2008 Richard Thaler and Cass Sunstein wrote a book (*Nudge*) in which they advocated that the government should give people a "nudge" in the right direction (libertarian paternalism.). The nudge would be to provide people with a default option, which was better than other choices, but allow them to opt out of the default option. Based on the psychology used by this book, they thought that people were more likely to stay with the default rather than making a choice to opt out because opting out requires a deliberate choice against the norm. (Can you see the framing and anchoring here by Thaler/Sunstein?) An example of a nudge would be having to opt out of making a contribution to an environmental fund on your taxes.

Of course, showing that it can be done, is not the same thing as saying it should be done. Should the government use paternalistic libertarianism, traditional libertarianism, or a regulatory state? There is no correct answer to this question.

One of the areas that government often regulates is false advertising. Should the government intervene when an advertiser uses cognitive biases to sell their products, as we saw in earlier examples?

Notes

1. *Wikipedia: List of Cognitive Biases.*

2. *Meteorologist Joe Bastardi Blasts Al Gore's Claims That Global Warming Caused Hurricane Sandy as "Stunningly Ignorant or Stunningly Deceptive."* [http://noisyroom.net/blog/2012/11/01/meteorologist-joe-bastardi-blasts-al-gores-claims-that-global-warming-caused-hurricane-sandy-as-stunningly-ignorant-or-stunningly-deceptive/]

3. Eugene Volokh, *Zero correlation between state homicide rate and state gun laws,* Washington Post (Oct. 6, 2015) [https://www.washingtonpost.com/news/volokh-conspiracy/wp/2015/10/06/zero-correlation-between-state-homicide-rate-and-state-gun-laws/?utm_term=.561a19c24711]

4. Based on Daniel Kahneman, Thinking, Fast and Slow 174-75 (2011). Based on Kahneman, *supra* at 174-75.

5. *Id.* at 182.

6. *Id.* at 105.

7. James Clear, *How to Spot a Common Mental Error That Leads to Misguided Thinking.* [http://jamesclear.com/illusory-correlation]

8. Kahneman, *supra* at 76.

9. *Id.* at 199.

10. *Id.*

11. *Wikipedia: List of Cognitive Biases.*

12. Kahneman, *supra* at 203.

13. Clear, *supra.*

14. Philip Fernbach & Steven Sloman, *Why We Believe Obvious Untruths*, New York Times (March 3, 2017). [https://www.nytimes.com/2017/03/03/opinion/sunday/why-we-believe-obvious-untruths.html?_r=0]

15. Philip Fernbach et,al., Political Extremism Is Supported by an Illusion of Understanding, Psychological Science (April 25, 2013). [http://www.meteo.mcgill.ca/~huardda/articles/fernbach13.pdf]

16. Stanford Encyclopedia of Philosophy: Analogy and Analogical Reasoning. [https://plato.stanford.edu/entries/reasoning-analogy/]

17. *Id.*

18. *Id.*

19. University College London, *Satnavs 'switch off' parts of the brain*, EurekAlert (March 21, 2017). [https://www.eurekalert.org/pub_releases/2017-03/ucl-so031617.php]

20. They mean literally expand–grow larger in size.

21. Cory S. Clements, Perception and Persuasion in Legal Argumentation: Using Informal Fallacies and Cognitive Biases to Win the War of Words, 2013 BYU L. Rev. 319, 320 (2013).

22. *Id.* at 319-20.

23. An independent clause can stand alone as a sentence; a dependent clause can't.

24. Clements, *supra*, at 354.

25. *Id.*

26. Kenneth D. Chestek, *Fear and Loathing in Persuasive Writing: An Empirical Study of the Effects of the Negativity Bias* (2017). [https://papers.ssrn.com/sol3/papers.cfm?abstract_id=2953996]

Special Topics

27. Noam Scheiber, *Uber Uses Psychological Tricks to Push Its Drivers' Buttons* (April 2, 2017). [https://www.nytimes.com/interactive/2017/04/02/technology/uber-drivers-psychological-tricks.html]

28. 60 Minutes, *What is "brain hacking"? Tech insiders on why you should care*, (April 9, 2017). [http://www.cbsnews.com/news/brain-hacking-tech-insiders-60-minutes/]

29. Clements, *supra*, at 359.

30. For example, a recent article in the Washington Post stated, "Unfortunately, there is little evidence that training reduces sexual harassment. Rather, training programs, along with anti-harassment policies and reporting procedures, do more to shield employers from liability than to protect employees from harassment." [https://www.washingtonpost.com/outlook/whats-the-point-of-sexual-harassment-training-often-to-protect-employers/2017/11/17/18cd631e-c97c-11e7-aa96-54417592cf72_story.html?utm_term=.7e7a361f11d2] The article continued, "There have been only a handful of empirical studies of sexual harassment training, and the research has not established that such training is effective. Some studies suggest that training may in fact backfire, reinforcing gendered stereotypes that place women at a disadvantage."

Similarly, an article in Time declared, "according to the Harvard Business Review, men who are found likely to harass women leave trainings sure that harassment is not a big deal." Time noted, "Those trainings tend to focus on helping people understand the rules, law, and procedure around harassment." [http://time.com/5032074/does-sexual-harassment-training-work-heres-what-the-research-shows/]

31. https://www.wired.com/story/many-startup-founders-doubt-extent-of-sexual-harassment/

32. Max H. Bazerman & Francesca Gino Toward a Deeper Understanding of Moral Judgment and Dishonesty, ANNUAL REVIEW OF LAW AND SOCIAL SCIENCE [https://dash.harvard.edu/bitstream/handle/1/10996807/bazerman_gino_beh-ethics-toward_annual-review_dec2012.pdf] at 22.

33. Ken Armstrong, *Power Point Justice*, https://www.themarshallproject.org/2014/12/23/powerpoint-justice.

34. Nos. 1-5 from Gus Lubin & Shana Lebowitz, *58 cognitive biases that screw up everything we do*, Business Insider (Oct. 29 (2015). [http://www.businessinsider.com/cognitive-biases-2015-10/#affect-heuristic-1] Nos. 6- from *Wikipedia: List of Cognitive Biases*. [https://en.wikipedia.org/wiki/List_of_cognitive_biases]

Chapter Nine
Review Exercises on Cognitive Biases

<u>Chapter Goals.</u>
1. To provide review exercises that will further refine your ability to spot and overcome cognitive biases.

Exercise: Giving Examples of Cognitive Biases

1. Go back to Chapter One and look at the list of biases. Think of at least one example of each bias.

Exercise: Recognizing Cognitive Biases

Label the following possible cognitive biases.

1. John has been dating Debbie for two years. He doesn't think that he and Debbie will get married, but he doesn't want to break up with her because of the time he has devoted to the relationship.
2. If our party doesn't win the election, the next four years will be a disaster.
3. Coach Sanchez said that the offense was playing well because of his coaching. However, he blamed the defense's struggles on his defensive coordinator.
4. Michelle thought that the department did not need reorganizing because the current set-up was better than the proposed alternatives.
5. Debbie thought that Rhonda Butler would be the best mayor over Troy Smith even though she hadn't read much about the election.
6. Marty staunchly supported the proposal when he learned that it would lower taxes, even though later he learned negative information about the proposal.
7. Larry applied to be head of the department even though he knew that most of his colleagues disliked him.
8. Pierre's favorite singer is Cathy Goodly. He thinks she must be a wonderful person.
9. I failed the exam because the other members of my study group didn't do a good job.
10. Bob is from Boston so we will take him out for scrod.
11. My friend is voting for the Democratic candidate because of her biases. I support the Republican candidate based on reasoning.
12. I am voting for that candidate because all my friends are.
13. All the evidence supports my theory. The negative evidence is unreliable.
14. We would have won the game if the coach hadn't punted on fourth down.
15. The police were wrong arresting my son for shoplifting. He would never commit a crime.
16. The quarter came up heads five times in a row. It must come up heads now.
17. I will pay you one thousand dollars now or two thousand dollars in a year. I'll take the thousand dollars now.
18. I can't understand why my boyfriend doesn't support my candidate for mayor. I have done more reading on the election than he has.
19. I think that the Martian candidate is better than the Venusian candidate. (You are Mar-

tian.)

20. I am really upset about the outcome of the election. All my friends must feel the same way.
21. All Martians are lazy.
22. Although Mike is still only the second clarinet in the college orchestra in his senior year, he believes he can get a job with a top professional orchestra when he graduates.
23. The company had spent two years and two million dollars at trying to develop the property for which they paid ten million dollars, without success. A buyer wants to purchase the property for ten million dollars. The company does not want to sell.
24. If I fail the test, my life will be ruined.
25. He is a terrible person because he smokes.
26. I have always been a poor learner; I will always be a poor learner.

Answers

1. Sunk-cost fallacy.
2. Dichotomous thinking or catastrophizing.
3. Self-serving bias.
4. Status-quo bias.
5. In-group bias.
6. Anchor bias.
7. Ostrich effect.
8. Halo effect.
9. Blaming.
10. Essentialism.
11. Bias-blind spot.
12. Bandwagon effect.
13. Confirmation bias or Semmelwis reflex.
14. Hindsight bias.
15. Subjective validation.
16. Gambler's fallacy.
17. Hyperbolic discounting.
18. Curse of knowledge.
19. In-group bias.
20. Projection bias.
21. Labeling or essentialism.
22. Optimism bias.
23. Sunk-cost fallacy.
24. Catastrophizing.
25. Dichotomous thinking or negative halo effect.
26. Fixed mindset.

You may have some different answers to a few of these because the cognitive biases overlap.

Review Exercises on Cognitive Biases

More Exercises

Identify the problems in the following.

1. I just read that there are no tigers in the wild in Africa. When is someone going to do something about global warming?
2. This evening, a string quartet is playing at the Arts Center downtown about 25 minutes away. The National Weather Service has predicted a significant snow storm for this evening. Who is more likely to attend this concert–a person who really likes this group but who hasn't bought a ticket or a person who purchased a ticket a month ago?
3. You need to buy a child seat for your car. Which one do you buy–a cheap seat that gives your child good protection or one that costs three times as much and provides 10% more protection to your child?
4. Winning this bid is important to the continuing viability of our company. I'm sure I can put together the winning bid.
5. The coach should have started Morgan. Not starting him cost us the game.
6. I'm starting tonight. We are sure to win.
7. This stock did very well last year. I'm going to buy it.
8. It's my mother's fault that I never accomplished anything.
9. If I don't get this job, my life is over.
10. I don't understand why my students can't solve the problem. It is an easy one.
11. I used to think he was a smart senator, but I changed my mind since he voted for the tax increase.
12. A tornado hasn't hit this area for fifty years. Why should we waste money preparing for something that isn't going to happen?
13. Don't let the fact that you lost your job bother you. When it happened to me I was fine.
14. I just know that my life is going to get worse.
15. I don't know what I'll do if I lose my job. Doris will probably leave me. I'll have to move into a smaller apartment, and I'll probably have to sell my car.
16. My publishing this article in the Harvard Law Review isn't important.
17. I estimate that we should be able to build this bridge in two years.
18. New Yorkers are smarter than Bostonians.
19. We don't need to change our curriculum. The one we have now works fine.
20. I've read the studies, but I still believe that childhood vaccination causes autism.
21. The car hit the plaintiff's vehicle at 30 mph. (versus) The car smashed into the plaintiff's vehicle at 30mph.
22. The dealer offered me $500 for my Chinese vase, but I am sure it is worth at least twice as much.
23. I know the proposal is bad because Larry made it.
24. The Kahneman study must be wrong. It contradicts all we know about rational actors.
25. The company is on the verge of bankruptcy, but its CEO is optimistic about the company's future.
26. All Martians are good singers.
27. Why can't my child learn to drive. It was easy for me.

28. While a couple of studies disagree, this study supports my thesis.
29. While our team is two touchdown underdogs, I am sure we will find a way to win.
30. I am responsible for the project's success.
31. I am proposing that we spend one billion dollars for peacekeeper missiles.

Answers

1. Here, the speaker is confusing correlation with causation. The reason there are no tigers in Africa is because tigers are not native to Africa. This example may be a little silly because it is so extreme, but it does show how many people see causation where there is none.

Of course, the fact that the speaker is wrong says nothing about whether global warming actually exists. What a global warming advocate needs to do is to present solid evidence that is not affected by cognitive biases. Such arguments are more convincing and less subject to attacks.

2. The person who already has a ticket. This is an example of loss aversion.
3. Of course, you buyer the safer seat. What parent doesn't want to protect their child as much as possible. But, is this the best decision from an objective point of view? Could you have used the money you saved on the seat to better protect your child in other areas, such as child proofing your house? Wider frames usually produce more rational decisions.
4. Overconfidence bias. What the speaker is missing is that he can't control the competitors' bids.
5. Hindsight bias.
6. Illusion of control.
7. Gambler's fallacy. Yes, stocks are a gamble. Availability heuristic.
8. Blaming.
9. Catastrophizing.
10. Curse of knowledge.
11. Dichotomous thinking.
12. Normalcy bias.
13. Empathy gap.
14. Fortune telling.
15. What if?.
16. Discounting positives.
17. Planning fallacy. Probably only considered the best case scenario.
18. In-group bias.
19. Status-quo bias.
20. Subjective validation.
21. This is the framing effect, using a loaded word. Using smashed, rather than hit, affects the hearer's emotions.
22. Endowment effect.
23. Reactive devaluation.
24. Semmelweis reflex.
25. Ostrich effect.
26. Essentialism.

Review Exercises on Cognitive Biases

27. Curse of knowledge.
28. Confirmation bias.
29. Optimism bias.
30. Self-serving bias.
31. Framing effect by using loaded word (peacekeeping). Politicians do this alll the time.

Exercises: Dangers of Cognitive Biases

What are the potential dangers of these cognitive biases.

1. I just can't learn. It's that simple.
2. Vaccinations cause autism.
3. Not preparing for a hurricane.
4. We've already spent two million dollars on this project. I'm not going to let a few setbacks stop us.
5. I can only use this hammer for hammering.
6. I know I've just started doing this, but I can walk a high wire without a net.

Comment

1. This is the fixed mindset. The danger here is the person will stop trying.
2. The danger here is that parents won't get their children vaccinated, and preventable, childhood diseases will spread.
3. The danger is that the government won't be prepared for a disaster when it hits.
4. Sunk-cost fallacy. The danger is spending money on a project that will fail. For example, your company has spent two million dollars on a project that will fail. It can spend another two million on the project and end up losing four million dollars. Or, it can spend the two million on a project that will succeed, and it will only lose two million. Of course, the alternatives are usually not as clear as in this example. Any analysis must consider all factors. The point, however, is that the sunk-cost fallacy should not be part of the decision-making process.
5. Functional fixedness limits creativity.
6. Death.

Extended Exercises

When you reach a letter, discuss the possible cognitive biases and solutions. If you are having trouble, consult the list of cognitive biases in Chapter One.

1. Meeting of Faculty Hiring Committee.

    Committee chair: We have three candidates for this position. Discussion?
    Dimitri: I think we should eliminate candidate A from consideration. He clerked for Justice Smith, and Justice Smith is a libertarian. [A] A libertarian won't fit in with this faculty. [B]

Understanding and Overcoming Cognitive Biases for Lawyers and Law Students

Liz: I read an article he wrote in which he opposed same-sex marriage. He is definitively very conservative. [C]

Dimitri: See! [D]

Roger: Maybe having a conservative on our faculty will be good for the students.

Dimitri: Bah! All conservatives are poor scholars, and they don't know how to dress. [E] I know everyone here agrees with me. [F]

Joan: If we don't hire professors with a wide-variety of ideologies, not enough students will sign up for our offerings, and the Dean will shut our department down. [G]

Trayvon: Remember, before I was on this committee, you refused to hire Professor Jackson on similar grounds, and now he is at Harvard. You made a big mistake there. [H]

Chair: What about candidate B?

Liz: She was Secretary of Commerce under the last administration so I think she will be the best teacher and scholar. [I]

Roger: Candidate C wrote that great article on corporate governance. [J]

Dimitri: Yes, but he wrote that awful article on Title Nine. [K]

Roger: That article was written before he got his first appointment. I wouldn't worry about it. [L]

Chair: We've been meeting for a couple of hours. Let's take a ten minute break. [M]

2. Assume you are in high school and you are deciding where to apply to college and filling out college applications.

I really don't want to do this. Mom is forcing me. I can wait until the weekend; they aren't due until Monday. [A] I don't know why I am doing this anyway; I'm too stupid to go to college. [B] I know Mrs. Wallace wrote me a good recommendation, but she probably does that for everybody. [C] I made mostly As in math courses, but you need more than math to succeed in college. [D] Anyway, I probably won't fit in. I'll be by myself every weekend in my dorm room. [E] Remember that time at Gail's party where I made a fool of myself. [F] Anyway, a lot of people in high school don't like me. [G] Anyway, I can't go to state college. It's two hours away from home. What if I get sick or have an anxiety attack? My parents won't be able to reach me in time. [H] Of course, this isn't really my fault. My parents are way too strict. [I]

3. This scenario is a meeting of the local planning board concerning a new water main.

Boss: First, I want to thank everyone for coming. I apologize for the mix-up concerning lunch. My email should have said to bring your own lunch. Anyway, we should be done around two so you can eat then. [A] First, we will hear from Tony about cost and completion time.

Tony: Okay, I've done the estimates, and the project should cost around five million and take nine months to complete. If we start in March . . . [B]

Tonya: Excuse me but how certain are you of those estimates?

Tony: 100%. I spent a long time going over the numbers. [C]

Tonya: Didn't Hillsdale do a similar project that had a 75% cost overrun?

Review Exercises on Cognitive Biases

Tony: Yes, but their planning board is not as good as ours. [D]

Tonya: I still don't think we've done enough analysis on cost and completion time.

Aside: Angela to Mark: There she goes again. I just dislike Tonya so much. She never knows what she is talking about. [E]

Tony: Just let me take care of it. Men are better than women with numbers. [F]

Boss: Let's hear what everyone else has to say. [G]

Long discussion

Boss: Okay, let's vote on whether to accept Tony's report.

Tonya (a little agitated): I just want to warn everyone. If we are wrong on our estimates, we'll all get fired, and we probably won't get jobs in this economy. [H]

Aside: Angela to Mark: I'm certainly not voting with Tonya. [I]

Proposal passes.

Boss: The motion passes. Good job everyone. I'll oversee the project, and everything will go fine. [J]

4. Same scenario; a year later.

Boss: Let's get started. As you all know the recent flood overloaded the sewerage system. This is the first time we've had a flood this big. [A] The construction company started the new sewer main, but it isn't going to be big enough now that we know about the possibility of large floods. We've spent three million on it, but it will take another five million to complete it. We could do a new sewer main near Echo Trail that will cost seven million.

Jack: I wish I had been on this committee when you approved this project. Anyone could have seen that the original pipe was too small. [B]

Boss: Well, let's not cry over spilt milk. [C]

Tonya: I warned you, but now we're stuck with fixing the original plan. We are already half done with construction. Anyway, if we don't complete the original project, we'll get blamed. [D] If I have nervous break down, it's all you fault. [E]

Jack: Suck it up Tonya. Let's not let unlikely things get in our way. [F]

Jin: I think we should look at this problem based on final cost. Starting over would save money. [G]

Pat: You know, there is that abandoned railroad tunnel. Maybe we could use that to save some on the new main.

Jin: You can't use a railroad tunnel to transport water. [H]

Tony: How long will each alternative take? [I]

Boss: That's enough for today. Think about it, and we can make a final decision next week.

5. Prom committee meeting.

Marcia: Let's get started. Everyone is in favor of holding it at the Biltmore Hotel downtown so we can just skip this item. [A]

Jackson: Slow down. Some people want to hold it here in our gym because it would be cheaper.

Marcia: Everyone I've talked to wants to hold it at the Biltmore. [B]

Jackson: No that isn't true; some students wouldn't be able to go if we hold it downtown.

Marcia: If you're talking about the rural kids, none of us cares. They don't fit in with us anyway. [C]

Mark (aside to Roberto): I'm sure Marcia's right. She's the prettiest girl in school. [D]

Angela (aside to Caitlin): I'm voting for the Biltmore; I can't stand that do-gooder Jackson. [E]

Jackson: I think you are a little prejudiced against the rural kids, Marcia. Some of my best friends are farm kids.

Marcia: How dare you accuse me of being biased. Our family buys all our vegetables at the Farmer's Market. [F]

Marcia: Okay let's vote. Who wants to hold the prom at the Biltmore Hotel downtown or our cruddy gym. [G]

Roberto [aside to Mark]: I'm voting for the Biltmore because everyone else is. [H]

Marcia: Okay, the Biltmore wins.

Jackson (yelling): I hope everyone is happy. None of the rural kids will go, and the principal will be mad. She might even cancel the prom. [I]

Marcia: No she won't. I'll keep the costs down in other ways. [J]

Discussion

1.

A. Anchoring or availability heuristic. Dimitri is making his decision based on too little evidence.
B. In-group bias.
C. Again, the availability heuristic.
D. Confirmation bias.
E. Dichotomous thinking and essentialism.
F. Dimitri is projecting his values and ideas on others. Also, mind reading.
G. Catastrophizing.
H. Hindsight bias.
I. Halo effect. The fact that she was Secretary of Commerce says nothing about being a teacher or a scholar.
J. Anchoring, availability heuristic, or mere-exposure effect.
K. Do you think Dimitri might have a negative filtering bias?
L. Expectation bias.
M. Good idea. The members can eat something so they can stay alert and think clearly.

2.

A. You are letting your emotions control your decision-making process. Procrastination is often a poor way of delaying things when you are emotional. To overcome your procras-

Review Exercises on Cognitive Biases

tination, promise yourself a reward. "When I finish these, I'll call Judy, and we can go to a movie." Also, think about the positive things about going to college.

B. You are labeling yourself. Reflect on why you are doing this. Are you really stupid? Probably not. Think about all the successes you had in high school.

C. Inability to disconfirm. Ask yourself why your teacher wrote the letter. Does she write good recommendation letters for bad students? Probably not. "Hey, maybe she really thinks I'm smart." Picture her writing the letter.

D. Discounting positives. If you are good at math, maybe you can major in math in college. Find what you can succeed at rather than focusing on the negatives.

E. Catastrophizing, fortune-telling. You are looking at the worst case scenario. Consider the good social things that can happen in college. Picture yourself being a social success.

F. Overgeneralizing. You are taking one event and thinking it will happen many times. Have you ever done this again? No. Then, why are you worrying. Also, realize that everyone makes mistakes. Furthermore, look at it from another's viewpoint. Do you think anyone other than you remembers the incident?

G. Negative filtering. Overgeneralizing. Nobody is loved by everyone. Focus on the friends you have, not those who aren't your friends.

H. What if? bias. Think about the alternatives. Don't colleges have health services to handle these kinds of problems?

I. Blaming. Take responsibility for yourself. If you don't, you will never grow into an adult.

3.

A. Big mistake. You should never make important decisions when you are hungry, tired, or angry. These conditions make it more likely that you will rely on your System 1 rather than your System 2.

B. Do you see a possible planning fallacy here? What would you do to overcome it?

C. Overconfidence effect.

D. Overconfidence effect, expectation bias, in-group bias.

E. Labeling.

F. Oh boy! Essentialism. Also, Tony's comments are likely to raise the emotional level of the room. The boss should say something here to cool things down. What would you do?

G. It would have been good to have everyone write down their opinions before the meeting so they don't become biased by others.

H. Catastrophizing.

I. Reactive devaluation.

J. Illusion of control, related to overconfidence effect. Nobody can control everything.

4.

A. Normalcy bias; the "Black Swan."

B. Hindsight bias.

C. Bad analogies don't help. While you shouldn't beat yourself up about failure, you need to learn from the failure.

D. Sunk-cost fallacy. This bias is especially a problem when the planners have an interest in the sunk cost. The key to solving this is to give it to another committee. (Of course, this might cause different problems.)
E. Blaming. Might Tonya's emotional problems may be due to something else.
F. Empathy gap.
G. Jin is trying to reframe the problem to overcome the sunken-cost fallacy.
H. Functional fixedness.
I. Tony is trying to reframe the problem.

5.

A. Mind reading or projection. Marcia is assuming that everyone feels the same way she does.
B. Confirmation bias, expectation bias, or semmelweis reflex. Marcia only pays attention to information that supports her preference.
C. In-group bias. Our group matters more than the rural kids.
D. Halo effect. The fact that she is pretty doesn't mean that Marcia is right.
E. Reactive devaluation.
F. Bias-blind spot.
G. Framing effect. The best way to win an argument is to be the one that frames the question, even if it is a little obvious here. You might have also said the anchoring effect. The discussion didn't get into a lot of details.
H. Band-wagon effect.
I. Emotional reasoning and catastrophizing.
J. Illusion of control. Others, such as merchants and caterers, have a large effect on the price. There is also overconfidence here, which usually accompanies illusion of control.

Chapter 10
Review Exercises on Cognitive Biases and Your Professional Life

<u>Chapter Goals.</u>
1. To provide review exercises that will further refine your ability to spot and overcome cognitive biases in your professional life.
2. To have you scrutinize the effect of cognitive biases on your professional life.

Review Exercises: Spotting Cognitive Biases

1. Write down all the ways that cognitive biases can interfere with the attorney-client relationship. (brainstorm) Look at this question from both viewpoints–attorney and client. Consider the scope of representation and allocation of authority between attorney and client. How can you avoid problems in these areas? How will you deal with a client who is suffering from cognitive biases? (Hint: don't confront them directly. They will get angry if you accuse them of having a cognitive bias.)
2. Write down all the ways that cognitive biases interfere with the interaction between opposing attorneys. (brainstorm) Think how overcoming these problems help clients and the public good.
3. Think how cognitive biases affect the adversarial system. How can some of these problems be overcome? Does having an adversarial system help get at the truth since opposing attorneys can point out the otherside's cognitive errors?
4. How do cognitive biases affect negotiations? (brainstorm) Would knowledge of cognitive biases by both parties help make negotiations more efficient?
5. Would knowledge of cognitive biases make our criminal justice system fairer? How? How do cognitive biases affect prosecutors? Defense attorneys? Criminals? Why do the model rules include special duties for prosecutors?
6. You are writing a contract for a sale of a building by your client. How might cognitive biases affect you?
7. You are writing a will for a client. How might cognitive biases affect you? A long-term, rich client wants you to draft an estate plan for his parents. He has two siblings as well as several other relatives. How might cognitive biases affect you?
8. A husband and wife want you to draw up a property settlement for their uncontested divorce. No other attorney is involved. Is this a good idea?
9. Two clients want you to write a contract for a sale of a business from one of the clients to another. Is this a good idea? What problems might arise if one of the clients is a long-term client and the other one is a new client?
10. Can an attorney represent two clients in the same bankruptcy proceeding? Can informed consent get rid of any problems?
11. Write down all the ways that cognitive biases might affect an in-house counsel. (brainstorm) How can you avoid these problems?
12. Write down all the ways cognitive biases might affect a government lawyer? (brainstorm) A DOJ lawyer? An EPA lawyer? An FTC lawyer? A lawyer for a state agency? Etc.

13. Consider the possible cognitive biases in this scenario: You have a general practice in a small town. You are also the city attorney.
14. How might cognitive biases affect the following ethical duties: a. competence, b. diligence, c. communications with clients, d. confidentiality of information, e. safekeeping property, f. meritorious claims and contentions, g. candor to the tribunal, h. fairness to opposing party and counsel?
15. How does representing an organization as a client differ from representing the individual officers of a corporation?
16. Lawyers are sometimes hired by a client to write an evaluation for a third-party. How do cognitive biases affect this?
17. Why are lawyers generally disqualified to be counsel for a party when they might be called as a witness?
18. Why do the model rules generally forbid lawyers and law firms from sharing fees with nonlawyers? Do you think this is a good rule?
19. Why do the model rules forbid a lawyer from forming a partnership with a nonlawyer for the practice of law?
20. How do cognitive biases affect other aspects of your practice, such as your relationship with employees, relationships with court personnel, paying bills, etc.? How do cognitive biases affect the running of a large law firm?
21. How do cognitive biases affect an attorney in his business dealings with others? Should an attorney go into business with a client? How does an attorney's special knowledge affect her relationship with business partners?
22. Regulation of attorney advertising has been controversial for many years. Does knowledge of cognitive biases change your viewpoint on attorney advertising?
23. Should an attorney be allowed to solicit clients at the court house? Should an attorney be allowed to visit a person who was injured in a car accident at the hospital?
24. An attorney is not required to accept all clients who request representation. Why is this a good rule?
25. Why do the model rules encourage lawyers to do pro bono? Are cognitive biases involved in whether you do pro bono?
26. Why do the model rules require that an attorney report another attorney's professional misconduct? Is this a good rule? How are cognitive biases involved? Did your university or law school have a similar rules concerning cheating? How can pro bono help an attorney overcome the in-group bias?
27. Does knowledge of cognitive biases and methods to overcome them increase an attorney's satisfaction with her professional life?

Review Exercises: Overcoming Cognitive Biases

1. How can an attorney overcome the overconfidence bias? Think of a problem in your law practice that was affected by the overconfidence effect, and think about how to overcome it.
2. How can an attorney overcome the Semmelweis effect? Did you ignore or downplay contradictory evidence in your practice? What have been the results?
3. How can an attorney stop blaming others for her mistakes? Think of times when you suf-

Review Exercises on Your Professional Life

fered from blaming in your professional career. What problems did this cause?
4. How can you avoid labeling others? What problems does labeling cause?
5. How can you avoid the availability heuristic in a case? Has the availability heuristic ever caused you to lose a case because you ignored something material?
6. How can you overcome the framing effect? Has the framing effect ever affected you in litigation or in a negotiation?
7. How might the endowment effect influence a settlement concerning a taking of a residence? How can you overcome this?
8. How can you help your client overcome the sunken-cost fallacy?
9. How can you avoid emotional reasoning in making decisions? Think of times in your practice when emotional reasoning has caused you problems.
10. How can you avoid catastrophizing? Think of times you have suffered from catastrophizing? Did things really turn out that bad?
11. How has the planning fallacy affected something in your practice? For example, has litigation cost more than you originally estimated? Or, has a case taken long than you had planned? How can you avoid the planning fallacy?
12. Has the normalcy bias (black swan) ever affected a case you have been working on? How were you surprised? How can you overcome the normalcy bias?
13. How can you overcome the empathy gap with your clients? Has the empathy gap ever affected your relationship with a client?
14. How can you overcome the in-group bias? Has the in-group bias ever affected a relationship with a client?
15. How can you overcome a bias blind spot? Has a bias blind spot ever caused you a problem in your practice?
16. How can you avoid the bandwagon effect? Has the bandwagon effect ever affected the decision-making in your law firm?
17. Has the curse of knowledge ever caused you a problem with a client or a subordinate? How can you overcome the curse of knowledge?
18. Has the illusion of control ever affected you in your law practice? How can you overcome the illusion of control.
19. How can you overcome the anchoring effect? Has the anchoring effect ever affected the outcome of one of your cases?
20. Do you suffer from the gambler's fallacy in your practice?

Answers

I have given sample answers for each of the above questions. There are additional correct answers.

1. Consider all alternatives. Analysis problems step-by-step, rather than jumping to conclusions. Look at the problem from a different viewpoint.
2. Weigh all the evidence equally. Be able to explain conflicting evidence.
3. Recognize that making mistakes is not necessarily bad; you can learn from mistakes. Take responsibility for your own actions. If you don't, you will cause yourself lots of problems.

Understanding and Overcoming Cognitive Biases for Lawyers and Law Students

4. Look at the individual, not group characteristics. Those who label avoid real thinking. If you label everything, you never develop detailed thinking.

5. Make sure you have all the information. Weigh all information equally. Explain every relevant factor. Don't focus on ease of retrieval.

6. Consider all alternatives. Reframe the issue from the otherside. Look for loaded words and sequencing.

7. The owner will want more money. Get an independent estimate. However, your client might still be hard to convince.

8. Do a cost-benefit analysis. If dealing with a company, suggest that a different manager make the decision.

9. Slow down. Perform a step-by-step analysis. Put off the decision if you are angry, hungry, or tired.

10. Do a careful analysis, rather than relying on your emotions. Talk to a friend.

11. Avoid being overly-optimistic. Designate a devil's advocate for your group. Determine how much time similar projects have taken (or cost) in the past. Estimate the time for subtasks and add them up.

12. Visualize possible outcomes. Look for alternatives. Think outside the box. Avoid simple answers.

13. Try to put yourself in their shoes. Try to visualize what your client is going through. Don't assume everyone feels the same emotions you do.

14. View people as individuals. Rely on judgment, rather than heuristics. Create cross-groups. Break down or eliminate categories.

15. Recognize that you have as many biases as the average person.

16. Avoid bowing to peer pressure. Consider all alternatives, rather tha making a snap decision based on the bandwagon effect.

17. Recognize that other people do not have the same level of knowledge and experience that you do in your field. Put yourself in the other person's shoes.

18. Recognize that other people may also have an effect on a situation.

19. Realize that the anchoring effect might be affecting your decision. Look to see whether the anchor is real or arbitrary. Make sure you have all the information.

20. Understand causation. Don't connect unconnected events. Think of the consequences of the gambler's fallacy.

Review Exercises: Behavioral Legal Ethics Review

1. Do you see how behavioral legal ethics (bounded rationality) gives a more complete picture of legal ethics than traditional legal ethics?
2. Do you understand how and why ethical blindness is a major cause of ethical lapses?
3. What are some of the causes of ethical blindness?
4. How does framing affect ethical blindness?
5. Why is it difficult for a lawyer to be objective?
6. What is the difference between the "pragmatic self" and the "idealistic self"?
7. What is faulty emotional prediction?
8. What is situational ethics?

Review Exercises on Your Professional Life

9. How can the context affect ethical conduct?
10. How does the bias blind spot affect a lawyer's ethics?
11. What is the slippery slope, and how can it affect legal ethics?
12. What are scripts, and how can they affect legal ethics?
13. How does the dread of realizing you have made a mistake affect legal ethics?
14. How can the overconfidence effect affect legal ethics?
15. What other biases affect legal ethics?
16. How do cognitive biases affect the subordinate-supervisory attorney relationship?
17. How do group dynamics affect legal ethics?
18. How does the use of an intermediary affect ethics?
19. Can the methods of behavioral legal ethics be applied to business ethics?
20. Can the methods of behavioral legal ethics be applied yo medical ethics?
21. Can the methods of behavioral legal ethics be applied to politics?

Final Problem

Write down the ten cognitive biases that you think affect you the most. Come up with a plan for avoiding these biases. Has reflection become part of your intellectual arsenal? Do you evaluate (learn from your mistakes and the mistakes of others)? Do you use self-monitoring while you are problem-solving? Do you use practical reasoning when dealing with ethical problems?

CPSIA information can be obtained
at www.ICGtesting.com
Printed in the USA
LVHW010430201218
601172LV00010B/183

9 781985 130135